Living Again

William Wallace's *Living Again* does a marvelous job of imparting hope that there is life again after a spouse's death. He provides an invaluable "road map" in identifying and constructively dealing with the traps along the road to recovery. As he so accurately observes, these traps can be avoided and he uses his own experiences in grief work so that others can move positively through their grief journey. I highly recommend this book as "must" reading for anyone who has lost a spouse.

> Paul J. Neal, Ph.D.
> Clinical Psychologist
> Christian Psychological Center

Living Again, born from the depths of William's pain and the triumph of renewal, cuts to the very heart of the emotion of loss and survival. Through his gift of reflective observation, William wraps surviving spouses into a kinship with a common bond as only someone who has "been there" can do. His words, though sometimes aching, raw, and tender, are always honest and thought-provoking; his advice, practical, insightful, and comforting. He manages to touch survivors exactly where they are with a promise of joy that comes with *Living Again*.

> Wallene Dockery Barzizza
> Author, Motivational Speaker, and
> Co-founder of FORWARD, a
> support group for surviving spouses

Published by Addax Publishing Group
Copyright © 1998 by William Wallace
Edited by Michael McKenzie
Designed by Randy Breeden
Cover Design by Jerry Hirt

For Information address:
Addax Publishing Group
8643 Hauser Drive, Suite 235, Lenexa, KS 66215

ISBN: 1-886110-49-2

Distributed to the trade by Andrews McMeel Publishing
4520 Main Street
Kansas City, MO 64111

1 3 5 7 9 10 8 6 4 2
Printed in the United States of America

Library of Congress Cataloging-in-Publication Data

Wallace, William, 1950-
    Living again : a personal journey for surviving spouses / by William Wallace.
      p. cm.
    ISBN 1-886110-49-2 (alk. paper)
    1. Bereavement—Psychological aspects. 2. Bereavement—Religious aspects—Christianity. 3. Grief. 4. Grief—Religious aspects-
-Christianity. 5. Spouses—Death—Psychological aspects. 6. Loss
(Psychology) I. Title.
BF575.G7W343 1998
155.9'37—dc21   97-51905
                                              CIP

Living Again

A Personal Journey for
Surviving the Loss of a Spouse

by William Wallace

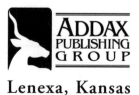

ADDAX
PUBLISHING
G R O U P

Lenexa, Kansas

Dedication

Dedicated to the memory of

Jada Wallace

September 6, 1949 - February 26, 1995

Table of Contents

Acknowledgements

Although writing this book seemed to be a solitary activity, it was in fact a collaborative effort. I drew from the experiences, associations, friendships, and relationships of a lifetime, each adding a brushstroke to the canvas of my life story.

Surviving the grief process and beginning to live again takes any surviving spouse on a personal journey from the despair of the loss, to the roller coaster ride of the present, and finally to the attainable potential of the future. Success on that journey depends in large part on how well we use three critical tools:

Faith, Family, and Friends.

While I am thankful, and wish to gratefully acknowledge the contribution of all who have touched my life, I would be remiss if I didn't recognize the contributions of those without whom the completion of this book would not have been possible.

- ❖ To God the Father for His patient love. To God the Son for His sacrifice. To God the Holy Spirit for His guidance and inspiration.

- ❖ To my mother, Florine, and my late father, Arthur, for providing living examples of the value structure that has provided the foundation for my growth and development.

- ❖ To my deceased wife Jada's family—Cy, Vaudean, and Kim—for continuing to share their family with me.

- ❖ To my sister, Sandra, my brother, Phillip, and their respective families for their loving support.

- ❖ To my extended family of aunts, uncles, and cousins who have truly demonstrated the meaning of family.

- ❖ To my Circle of Friends, who showered me with genuine caring, love, and support.

- ❖ To all the members of the Forward grief support group, who not only showed me the path to recovery, but walked it with me.

- ❖ To Michael McKenzie who through his professional editing brought this book to life.

- ❖ To my children—Charlie, Chris, and Chad—for continuing to remind me that while the body of our deceased loved one is gone, memory of her lives on.

Introduction

My wife died February 26, 1995, at the end of our 17th year of marriage. Therefore, I have at least some level of understanding about what anyone is going through in coping either with the loss of a spouse, or with knowing that his or her death appears imminent. My heart goes out to you and your family as your journey begins.

I have lived the American dream most of my life, well-educated, upwardly-mobile, financially-secure, married, three healthy children, nice home, great job. By any standard I would be considered successful. What more could I ask for? Yet, when my wife, Jada, was diagnosed with cancer, and I watched the slow, agonizing progression toward her death, my successes no longer mattered.

All of the positives were overshadowed by the mind-numbing negative of facing the remainder of my life without the one I loved.

Wading into the first anguishing months of grief recovery, and forced to face the realities of my loss, I sought help from an array of grief recovery materials. Each was tidily outlined, well-intentioned, but as cold as the paper on which they were printed.

I wanted an operational manual that would speak to me heart-to-heart. I found none. That dearth of gut-level information, plus the healing experience of journal-keeping (which we will discuss in detail), led me to you with this offering, straight from my healing heart to the ache in yours.

Side by side, I will discuss with you what you must do and how to pull through a bleak experience, to overcome a mound of powerful, draining emotions, to survive the harsh push-pull of death, and to emerge into a state of living again. I mince no words on this delicate subject. There is no way to make easy the pain or the path.

We know that none of us is immortal. We know this from start to finish. At some point in time we shed our bodily shells, and our spirits leave this life for the next. Yet, married couples spend significant portions of time together planning for a future that seems boundless, timeless, endless.

We speak the words, "until death do us part," as a matter of course, borne of tradition. But perish the thought. That concept is buried in the recesses of our dreaming minds as the euphoria of love and partnership and companionship consumes us.

Jada liked to refer to our long-term plans and dreams as our retirement together to the rocking chairs on the front porch.

When that image shatters, scattered in sharp, piercing shards, your stage of life and marriage matters very little – 30, or 80, or whatever age. Those dreams and hopes, the life that you built together for two, must now be occupied by one.

Introduction

We are ill-prepared for that shocking reality.

Words alone fall short of adequate description of the hurt, the pain, the sense of hopelessness and helplessness that consumes your heart when you lose a spouse. Even the heartfelt expressions of sympathy and support forthcoming from families and friends ring hollow as they attempt to provide a measure of comfort.

Life's experiences prepare us to cope with many things, including some preparation for the death of a loved one. But we can do so little to prepare for the grief we feel when that death occurs.

The loss of a spouse causes dramatic and immediate change in every part of your life, affecting, usually threatening, the very fabric of your existence. Each person brings very special qualities to the marriage union. If you are like me, and I imagine that most people are, you took for granted so much of what your spouse provided.

You perhaps never realized or appreciated just how much your spouse brought to the partnership. Unfortunately, in grimness and probably tugged by regret and guilt, now you are discovering how significant those contributions were.

Today the thought of living again might seem quite foreign to you. "Who cares?" you might ask. But I believe strongly that at some point in the near future, as you progress through the grief process, you will want to move beyond surviving your grief. I pray that this book will help you find the path you are seeking.

The concepts, drawn from my personal experience of losing Jada to an agonizing and extended illness, helped pull me through the complex web of feelings and reactions and duties, to a point of living again. To a point of where I am capable of loving and being loved again. To a point that results in marrying again.

The concepts of *Living Again* will guide you, but this is not a book in which you find a list of shortcuts to hasten the end of the grief process and hasten to beginning life anew. Rather, you will gain a better understanding of what you can expect to experience on your journey through grief.

Beyond that, I offer comfort and assurance by example as you discover the possibility of restoring a full and richly rewarding life, even though that might not seem possible to you today.

Living with a spouse is like reading a good book. Whether the book contains many chapters or is relatively short, the pages turn through a wide range of human emotions – love, romance, happiness, sadness, fear, and joy, to name just a few. We hope that the marriage, like a good book, never ends, but eventually we come to the last page.

Oh, how we wanted to savor the plot, the hero and heroine, longer. Just one more page, please, one more day, hour, moment, before the light is turned off.

Every time, the story line ends far sooner than we wanted. Closing that wonderful book and beginning another is the essence of *Living Again*.

If you wish success in life, make perseverance your bosom friend, experience your wise counselor, caution your elder brother, and hope your guardian genius.

—Joseph Addison

Chapter 1
The Journey Begins with an Ending

Nobody chose this to happen. Death thrust this journey on us, and every person on the path has a story to tell about how fate put him there. Each story, however different, starts the same—with the ending of a spouse's life.

My journey toward becoming a widower began in earnest June 10, 1993, when a surgeon entered the room where I was waiting. He uttered chilling words: "It's cancer."

Jada had not felt well for quite some time. Spells came and went, but she brushed off the symptoms, mostly chronic fatigue, as attributable to her stress from raising three children and managing our household. I was too caught up in my career demands, and some problems in our marriage, to scarcely notice.

During May of '93, when Jada noticed a swelling under her right arm, only then did she make an appointment to see our family physician. He performed a mammogram, detected a mass in her right breast, and scheduled a biopsy for June 10.

The day began as a beautiful, sun-drenched day, typical of the late spring we had grown accustomed to since moving from Mississippi to Memphis in December of 1987. We went to Germantown Community Hospital for Jada's medical appointment.

As they wheeled her out of the waiting room we kissed and I told her how much I loved her. Little did we know that within a few, short hours our worst fears would be realized.

Throughout the wait I felt the same restlessness I experienced during the birth of our children. Continuously I told myself that the mass would be benign, and I was convinced that this would come true if I said it often enough. Each time I thought of the possibility of cancer I quickly chastised myself for allowing such a negative thought to enter my head. We needed positive energy to make this ordeal become just another bad dream.

Minutes dragged like hours as I awaited some word from the doctor. I killed time reading old news magazines. When the phone rang, I jumped and almost fell out of the chair. The call was from the recovery room, saying that Jada had done well and would be returning to me shortly. The surgeon, they said, would be in to see me as soon as possible. After what seemed like an eternity the surgeon entered the room, dressed in typical, white doctor's garb.

I tried to read his face, but it told me nothing. And then in a quiet, almost genteel voice, he spoke the cold words that we pray we never will hear. In that instant I felt like I had been broad-sided, hit between the eyes with a two-by-four. A thousand questions rambled through my brain, yet stayed frozen in my throat, unasked.

Shock, fear, and the sense of this-can't-be-happening rushed over me. I hoped this news was simply a cruel joke, or a bad dream. Neither was true. I couldn't imagine a sunny day any darker.

The test results brought a diagnosis of metastatic breast cancer with massive lymph node involvement. Over the next 20 months Jada endured a continuous stream of diagnostic and treatment procedures – surgery, chemotherapy, radiation. Each bought her more time. None stopped the cancer from growing.

As she progressed through the various treatments I watched each one exact more toll on her physical and emotional state. We decided to keep the children informed about the disease, but to downplay the severity. In many ways we created a false sense of hope as the illness grew worse.

In December of 1994 Jada's oncologist informed us that the cancer had spread to her liver and lungs. I will never forget his words: "There is nothing else to do."

Jada's condition now was considered terminal. The doctor's advice to us was to radiate the largest of the new tumors, to place Jada on a program to minimize the pain, to go home, and to prepare for her death. The prognosis—how long she had—was unknown, but I had always believed that the verdict of terminal meant at least six months to put all affairs in order. I was soon to find out how naive I was about that.

Single-minded in purpose, she fought the disease hard. She read relentlessly any material she could get her hands on regarding possible treatment alternatives. Jada always believed that someone out there had experienced a worse case than hers, and survived. She wanted to know how.

Refusing to give up, we searched for another treatment facility where she might get help. We settled on Cancer Treatment Centers of America in Tulsa, Okla. Jada became a patient there February 13, 1995, still hoping against hope. Perhaps we were naive. Perhaps foolish. Or, perhaps just too scared to face the reality of what was happening to her, to us, to our family.

The reality was this: 13 days. Death inside of two weeks was her manifest destiny in Tulsa – many miles from home, and eons away from her rocking-chair retirement on the porch. After four days on life support, Jada died Sunday, February 26, 1995, one day after our 17th wedding anniversary. She was 45 years young, survived by a husband and three children—Charlie, 16, Chris, 11, and Chad, 7.

I decided to begin by recounting the story of Jada's death because I believe that to gain an understanding of where we are going, first we must understand – or at least come to terms with – where we have been. Before moving on, first we must close the door on the past. The formal term for this is closure. It is essential.

This figurative closing of a door is just that – closing, not slamming, not nailing it shut. Obviously we want and need a connection between the past and future. The closure takes place in a ritualistic manner, and allows us not only to begin building a future, but also to create a bridge that eventually spans past, present, and future.

Closing the door does not mean we will lock it up and throw away the key, never again to visit precious memories. Closure involves placing those memories into a healthy perspective, stored in an appropriate place. I found that by creating a special place in my heart for Jada, I increased the depth and breadth of my understanding of our relationship, and probably have done so with significantly less emotional pain.

I still visit with her often in my heart. Sometimes I cry, sometimes I laugh. Always, I come away feeling stronger.

Closing the pages on this chapter of your life – the death of your spouse – is difficult under the best of circumstances. When you are unsure, when fear grips tight and loneliness sweeps in, the closure is emotionally disturbing, deeply depressing. And it hurts.

Jada provided a cornerstone in my life. I did not want to close the door on her. At times I was uncertain that I could. Yet, in my heart of hearts, I knew closure was a necessary part of the healing process.

Earth hath no sorrow that heaven cannot heal.

—Thomas Moore

Chapter 2
Preparing to Close the Door

A common response upon the death of a spouse is a fortunate experience of numbness, blocking out the emotional pain. That numbness generally lasts a few days, or perhaps a few weeks, but inevitably the emotional pain sets in. The surviving spouse, consciousness jolted, is left to deal with making some sense out of what happened.

Comprehending Jada's death – what happened and why it happened – occurred for me on three levels:

❖ Spiritual.

❖ Intellectual.

❖ Emotional.

Spiritual understanding came first and easiest. In dealing with cancer, you always remain consciously aware that death is a possibility. Avoiding the specter of death is virtually impossible, and often you become caught up in discovering the bravado and inner strength to deal with it.

Living Again

As a Catholic Christian I believed throughout our ordeal that if I lost Jada it would be by God's will. My strong belief that spiritual life exists after death, coupled with the knowledge that Jada's belief in God assured her a place in His heavenly kingdom, provided a great source of strength.

However, even my firmly held beliefs about God's plan for our lives proved insufficient to quell my overwhelming emotions during the last days before and the first days after her death. I was unable to grasp why His plan called for this terrible disruption to our lives at this time. Didn't God see how much the children and I needed her, and how empty our lives would be without her?

After much prayerful thought I believe my heart was touched with an answer. God places each of us on this earth with a purpose, and when that purpose is complete He calls us home to our reward. Whether the gift of that purposeful life spans one day or 100 years is unimportant. Jada's life's work was finished, but mine and the children's continued, and although we know not what God has planned for us we find comfort in knowing that He will reveal His plan according to His timetable. In the words of an old church song, we attain the peace that passes understanding.

Yes, God understood how much our family needed Jada, and how empty our lives would be without her, but He promised that His love and strength would sustain us through our hour of need as it had sustained us throughout our lives.

Spiritual understanding is, I believe, at the core of the healing process. (Again, my belief is rooted in the Christian faith. The same principles apply in all other faith and belief systems and philosophies: gaining inner peace to withstand the darkest hours of life.)

Intellectual understanding came slower. While I understood that Jada had died and would not be coming back, several burning questions haunted me.

Why was there no medical cure for this disease? Why didn't the first surgeon we consulted perform a mastectomy rather than a lumpectomy? Or, was there some other treatment she should have received? Was there something else I could have or should have done?

I am sure you have asked similar questions specific to the circumstances surrounding your spouse's death. Is an answer always immediately forthcoming? No. Sometimes never. If you find answers, be thankful.

However, please realize that often the answers to such questions are unknown and unknowable. When questions of this nature arise I find that an obsessive pursuit of an answer creates negative energy which truly impedes me in moving forward. Pursue the answers to pervasive questions, if you must. Just know that at some point the pursuit could result in more harm than the good that might come from an answer.

Emotional understanding was, and, quite frankly, remains the most difficult level for me to deal with. Uneven emotions create the most variations in my behavior—variations best described as an emotional roller coaster. The peaks are those periods when the emotional pain momentarily subsides, and are characterized by a sense of euphoria. The valleys are those periods of intense emotional pain often characterized by fear, anger, and worry. You will find a more detailed examination of this subject in Chapter 6.

Striving for emotional peace caused me to search continuously deep inside myself to uncover my most personal feelings. The search touched the raw edges of my feelings and emotions.

Much of the emotional distress during the early stages of grief results from an identity crisis. Throughout married life we develop an identity blended with our mate's. To be successful in marriage each partner willingly gives up part of his or her individual identity, and in many ways marriage defines who we are. The loss of a spouse can cloud a person's identity to the point of asking, "Who am I now?"

As surviving spouses, we know we are not the same person we were before we married. In many ways we still feel married. Yet the death of our spouse makes us someone other than who we were during our marriage. The stress associated with the loss and the disassociation is magnified by the fear of the unknown future.

The search for and the development of a new identity is, in large part, what moving through grief and into living again is about.

Wouldn't life be wonderful if that passage could take place instantly—in a mentally and emotionally healthy way? Time heals, yes, but that altruism isn't completely comforting because the passing of time during the search for emotional understanding is painful.

When the pain seems overbearing, with no end in sight, take solace in knowing that the search for emotional understanding coupled with your spiritual understanding can, in time, create the greatest opportunity for personal growth.

Gradually gaining understanding on the three levels – spiritual, intellectual, and emotional – was a critical early step in the healing process for me after Jada's death. I also quickly found out it was only the beginning. Many more critical steps would follow.

I was confident that I could treat the grief process much the same way as a business problem. Why should this be any different than problems I had handled for years? It seemed as though it was all a function of planning, organizing, executing, and establishing a time line for completing the grief process.

Not so, as you soon will see.

We can do anything we want to do,

if we stick to it long enough.

—Helen Keller

Chapter 3
Time

I wish I could tell you that the pain you feel today will be gone in six months, or one, or three ... and then no more tears, no more sorrow, no more lonely days.

I can't.

How long after your spouse has died will you mourn, and hurt, in tumultuous confusion? When can you expect to begin feeling normal? And, please, please ... when will the emotional pain go away? These questions will haunt you time and time again. I'd love to offer a precise timetable for you.

No one can give an exact time.

Typically, family and friends who have not experienced anything like what you and I have in losing a spouse hold to an impression that we should have our lives back together in short order, within a few, quick months.

When they see a continuing struggle with emotional control or stability their first inclination usually is to say, "Get a grip," well-intentioned in advising you to put the past in the past, to quit feeling sorry for yourself and move on. Well-intentioned, perhaps, but misguided. You might hear this often enough that you begin to doubt yourself, and to wonder if something is wrong with you, to wonder why this recovery process is taking so long?

While it is true that time is the great healer, the grief process cannot be bound to a time line.

As much as you probably would like to move on, you simply must not force the process along any faster than you are emotionally prepared to handle. The grief process is full of traps, which will be covered in Chapters 6 and 7.

When you move through the process too fast, you impair your ability to recognize and avoid or deal with traps, causing you to spend far more time getting out of them than moving forward. I'm reminded here of a former business co-worker who, when he thought we were trying to move our organization too far too fast, frequently cautioned that in the Aesop's fable *The Tortoise and the Hare*, "The tortoise always won the race."

This analogy to the grief process reflects a secondary moral of the fable: a slow-but-sure approach reaches a goal faster. All too often, bolstered by a little success, the temptation sets in to look for shortcuts—ways to leap-frog steps in the process. Skipping steps in grieving can be both painful and time consuming, and let's face it, if you can save pain and time you most likely will stay the course.

While I don't believe there are any tried and true shortcuts, I do believe that just as traps line the recovery path, some powerful tools also are available to enhance the healing process.

As I began my journey to living again in 1995 I expected it to take considerable time. In retrospect, I truly was unprepared for how long the transformation would take. I operated under the false assumption that in six months my life should be back to normal. What I have come to understand is that I had the wrong perception of what normal should be.

The sense of normalcy I sought, and expected, was not possible. Normal, to me, was rooted in my life with Jada, and there would be no more life with Jada. Therefore, if I wanted a normal life again it would have to come from a newly-created state of normalcy.

Jada was gone and there was nothing I could do about it. She could no longer be an active participant in my life. I didn't have to like that, but I did need to acknowledge and understand that reality. Only then could I begin developing my new "normal," and to recognize that its development would evolve continuously over a long stretch of time.

A final point about this matter of time:

Initially I had a strong tendency to evaluate my progress on a daily basis. As you have probably already experienced, variation occurs widely from day to day in how we feel about ourselves and our lives without our spouse. One day, you sit on top the world; the next, you lapse into a state of mild depression, sometimes worse.

Constantly-changing highs and lows have a strong effect on measuring progress. To maintain a balanced perspective I sought not to worry about the day-to-day mood swings, although I must admit I wasn't always able to do so. I attempted to focus on the broader picture—how I was improving over time.

Living Again

I remind myself daily that I am better today than I was six months ago, but not nearly as well as I will be six months from now.

The pain doesn't stop, nor does the sorrow you feel go away on a given day, but a daily affirmation does provide a source of inner support and strength to help you know that you are on the right path. You create an inner voice that shouts, "I'm going to survive this!"

Affirmation Exercise

An affirmation is a positive statement of belief, a motto to live by. It is personal, and holds meaning only for the affirmed individual. Writing your affirmation, and then reciting it each morning, provides a powerful tool to prepare you to meet the challenges of each new day.

Write many affirmations. Keep them short and to the point.

Write an affirmation in first person, present tense, and as a positive.

Example: I think good thoughts.

Your Affirmation List

_____

_____

_____

_____

_____

_____

_____

_____

What we learn with pleasure, we never forget.

– Alfred Mercier

Chapter 4
The Common Ground of Grief

Each person who loses a spouse must take a demanding personal journey through a grieving process that at various times is overwhelming, sometimes paralyzing with its vise-like grip. Grief pounds at the human mind and spirit. Inner voices shout, "Life will never be okay again!"

That is common ground.

In many other ways the journey bears no commonality, because of the unique nature of each individual, and the unique aspects of the relationship he or she had with the deceased. No two identical situations can be found to handle exactly the same way, because of variables such as age, gender, spiritual maturity, children, circumstances surrounding the spouse's death, socio-economic background, and more.

To illustrate:

A 22-year-old widow who is a mother of three and has limited education has a far different-looking journey through grief to living again than a middle-aged, college-educated widow whose children are grown and who is on a career track.

I lost Jada to a prolonged illness. Someone else is jolted by a sudden, fatal heart attack or traffic accident. Our processes for grieving and rebuilding will have inherent variances.

No situation is easier or harder than another, just different in the nuances of the same difficult task of grief recovery and living again.

For all the differences among us, however, every surviving spouse walks some very common ground during the first year after the death of his or her spouse.

Common Grounds:

Special days you shared

- ❖ Deceased spouse's birthday
- ❖ Your birthday
- ❖ Children's birthdays
- ❖ Wedding anniversary
- ❖ Mother's Day
- ❖ Father's Day
- ❖ Valentines Day
- ❖ Anniversary of your spouse's death

Holidays prone to family traditions

❖ New Year's Day

❖ Easter

❖ Fourth of July

❖ Thanksgiving

❖ Christmas/Hanukkah (or other religious celebrations)

Special places that were "yours"

❖ Church

❖ Restaurants

❖ Theatres

❖ Parks

❖ Homes/Addresses

❖ Vacation spots

❖ Other places you lived or visited together

Activities

- ❖ Walks, running, or other exercise
- ❖ Drives in the country
- ❖ Movies, plays, concerts, etc.
- ❖ Entertaining company
- ❖ Talks about a certain subject, or life in general
- ❖ Hobbies

Instant reminders

- ❖ "Our song" or "our movie"
- ❖ Favorite lines he or she would say
- ❖ Clothing, such as a style of hat, or dress
- ❖ A laugh

I am sure you can add several to the list that have special meaning to you.

What is so significant about the common grounds during the first year after your spouse's death is that for the first time since you met and fell in love you will be experiencing them without her or him. A connection exists between a spouse and the items listed that evokes emotions in you.

The more significant the common ground was to you and your spouse, the more powerful the connection, and, as you experience these events for the first time alone, each will generate some level of emotional response.

Brace yourself; usually that emotional response is intense.

I experienced a good example shortly after Jada's death. Less than a month after the funeral our children were out of school for spring break, and we traveled by car to my parents' home in South Alabama for the week. We took our normal route from our home in Memphis, through Birmingham—a route we had taken countless times.

However this time as we approached Birmingham an energy-draining feeling came over me. It grew stronger as we made our way through the city. At first I couldn't comprehend why I was feeling this way. Then it dawned on me: Birmingham was where Jada and I had met on a blind date in November of 1977. I had proposed to her there, and Birmingham contained most of my early memories of our relationship.

In my wildest dreams I never would have thought about the powerful effect those memories would have on me. Recognizing the source of my feelings allowed me to prepare better for future, similar situations. I began anticipating my emotional reactions, and in so doing I reduced the frequency of emotional surprises I might otherwise have experienced.

Living Again

I want to emphasize that the Birmingham experience did not eliminate the emotional feelings about the significant events of our past as a couple, but that awakening greatly reduced the fear of experiencing similar links and remembrances.

This learning allowed me to use these common-ground experiences as a part of my healing—a process known as catharsis, defined as a purging of a complexity by bringing it to consciousness and giving it expression. In layman's terms, this means that you can derive strong, healing benefits from reviving the common-ground items and celebrating them, rather than avoiding them.

We know that we cannot avoid these common-ground experiences. But rather than fear them, lean into the discomfort they cause, and learn and grow from the experience. I found that the anticipated pain frequently was far greater than the actual pain. And as I prepared for each event I became adept at controlling my reaction, and thereby created a healing experience.

Cathartic Experience Exercise

Pick a common-ground special day or event you have yet to experience and complete the following exercise.

Special day or event:

_____

Describe what the day or event meant to you and your spouse:

_____

_____

Describe your feelings of anticipation:

_____

_____

What can you do to make this experience more bearable?

_____

_____

What could someone else do to help?

_____

_____

I have encountered these same feelings numerous times in the ensuing years. Although I am better prepared today to deal with each situation, and the frequency and intensity are diminished, they do still occur.

In many ways I was very fortunate that I had some time to begin the healing process before I had to deal with special days. Easter and Mother's Day were the first two, and, while they were significant, they were not as emotionally-charged as Jada's birthday, Thanksgiving, Christmas, or our wedding anniversary.

The emotional connection between the surviving spouse, the deceased, and the special days is among the most powerful. The memories of those occasions not only are vivid, but in all likelihood they represent many of the defining moments of your life together.

When my father passed away in August of 1996, my mother was forced to deal with special days almost immediately. Within the first four months she experienced his birthday in October, their wedding anniversary and Thanksgiving in November, and then Christmas in December. In a conversation we had during that first Christmas after Dad died, she told me that dealing with the special days had been among the most difficult and emotionally draining trials she had faced.

It made sense to me that the difficulty of getting through special days registers high at any time, but that difficulty becomes magnified even more for surviving spouses when those days confront them so early in the grief process.

The best way I found to travel the path across these nostalgic common grounds, and to cope with the emotions stemming from the recurring themes of togetherness you shared, was to anticipate rather than try to avoid the pain. Anticipation does not mean I looked forward to it joyfully, but acknowledged the pain as unavoidable. This anticipation allowed me to reflect on what the event or special day meant, and generated a new perspective regarding what was about to be experienced. The positive result was a less painful experience and ultimately less fear about future experiences.

For me that first Christmas without Jada, even though it was nearly a year after her death, was far and away the most difficult of all the common-ground experiences. My most vivid recollection occurred while our three children and I decorated the tree.

In our family, like many of yours, decorating the tree had become ritualistic, and I intended to maintain as many rituals as possible. The emotions began to well up when we four selected the tree, intensified as we decorated the branches with ornaments (most of which were hand-made by Jada), and culminated as I placed the angel on top and our youngest son, Chad, 8 years old at the time, looked at it and proclaimed:

"Look, that's mom."

Tears of joy, and of sadness, immediately welled up in my eyes. The simplistic beauty of that statement acknowledged Chad's belief that his mother could participate in our Christmas observance as an angel on our tree. That moment reminded me of the true meaning of Christmas, and I believe the children and I enjoyed the entire holiday season more than we would have otherwise.

Living Again

In addition to special days, often you encounter day-to-day events that you know your spouse would have enjoyed immensely. Perhaps your child is involved in a school or youth-group activity. Or, if the child is grown, possibly a rite of passage takes place — a wedding, or the birth of a grandchild. It might be, as my mother once described, simply just wanting to tell your missing spouse about something you saw or read.

Another vivid picture holds firmly in my mind from December of 1994, soon after Jada learned the terminal nature of her disease. She attended Chad's first-grade Christmas program at his school. She took great pleasure from the children's school activities. Upon returning home Jada was in tears. When I asked what had happened she said it came over her that this might have been the last program she would get to see. As it turned out, she was right. So when I attended Chad's second-grade program in 1995 I was very conscious of Jada not being present in person, and that remains among the saddest of times I have encountered since her death.

Another significant event took place when our oldest son, Charlie, was graduated from high school in May of 1996. This took place a full 15 months after Jada died, yet it was no less painful than many of the events that occurred during the first weeks, months, and year.

The situations I have shared brought to the surface two sides of me that I had rarely shown anyone, including myself: a sense of how unfair Jada's death was to her and to our children, and deep-seated anger over her being gone from us. For a long time I denied and suppressed my anger, and avoided acknowledging bitterness over how we all had been cheated.

I had difficulty getting past my belief that a mother should be able to see her children grow up, and that children should have their mother with them throughout their formative years. (Obviously this applies to fathers as well.)

While I cope with this better as time goes on, I still struggle, sometimes mightily, in the areas of the common grounds of grief.

In all things it is better to hope than to despair.

—Goethe

Chapter 5
Almost Ready

Y ou are virtually certain to face the experiences outlined in the previous chapters, and face them rather quickly in the grief process. You will conquer some of them in the truest sense of the word. You will release yourself from the powerful grip they hold on your mind and spirit.

In other situations, you might take solace in knowing they did not conquer you. That can be scored as a victory, too, if you will—a step forward, even if you are still dazed and confused, but not down and out.

You have begun distinctly to move forward now, gaining momentum and some level of confidence in your ability to create a new life. You have moved methodically through time, through closure, and into spiritual, mental, and emotional understanding.

The place where you stand at this point represents a time when I finally felt in control, when I believed that good things would happen, and happen quickly.

However, I encountered a great barrier.

The time was about six months after Jada's death. I thought I had made great strides, and was feeling quite good about myself. Then I noticed that I was not getting better, and, indeed, I was regressing.

Obviously, this was not good. This phase of my recovery was quite demoralizing and, to some extent, depressing. Here I was six months into the grief process and it was like I had run into a brick wall. For several weeks I tried to make sense of what was happening, but to no avail.

I finally realized, after much introspection and probing that I was experiencing guilt. It stemmed from the thought that maybe I was getting better too quickly, too easily. The question came to mind: Was getting better in some way being disrespectful to Jada's memory?

As I reflected on this question, and applied it to the grief process, another question arose—one that, while simple, is fundamental to living again:

What would Jada want for me?

I told you it was simple, but I'm sure you can see the power generated from the question, "What would your deceased spouse want for you?" And, moreover, in finding the answer.

My search for the answer to this question led to four beliefs about what Jada would want for me in her absence:

1. She would want me to focus on the good times we had together, and let go of the sad times, especially in that final year.

2. She would want me to raise our children to be spiritually, morally, and mentally prepared to become productive and happy adults.

3. She would want me to let go of any feelings of guilt I might have remaining from our time together.

4. She would want me to be happy.

A couple of points might easily be misinterpreted. To clarify:

This process is not like turning a light bulb on or off, although the way I have described it could leave that impression. Knowing and articulating what the deceased would want for you is only the first step.

Understanding this knowledge and then putting to use what you have learned is another step in the process to living again. (In the Appendix, use Exercise 5 to determine what your deceased spouse would want for you now.)

Once again, your understanding must develop spiritually, intellectually, and emotionally to make good use of the insights you have gained, and that takes time. For example, take the statement, "I should focus on the good times and let go of the sad times." Easy to say, hard to do.

There were days, even weeks, that I never consciously thought of the sad times. Yet there were days when I thought of almost nothing else. I doubted that I could ever let go of the sad times totally, but, over time, I learned to gain greater control (not total control) over sad thoughts and remembrances and how I chose to let them affect me.

Some elements of the answer to what the deceased would want for the surviving spouse might be vague or ambiguous, such as the first (or fourth) one. While finding happiness makes perfectly good sense, it lacks definition. What does it mean to be happy? Today it could mean not to despair in so much emotional pain. Tomorrow it could mean smiling or laughing. A year later it could mean something totally different.

As understanding grows, the ability to use that understanding in new and exciting ways grows as well. This process adds breadth and depth to the understanding, which in turn opens up opportunities for personal growth.

Your answer to the major question of what your spouse would want for you in his or her absence might be similar to mine, or perhaps it is totally different; either way, I believe that whatever the answer, it opens a window through which to see clearly one more piece of the process necessary to closing the door and to living again.

Hope is like the sun, which, as we journey toward it, casts the shadow of our burden behind us.

—Samuel Smiles

Chapter 6
Traps

O n the path toward living again, in creating that new state of normalcy, keep your eyes open for the traps along the way. Many of the traps are not bad, nor should you avoid them out of any sense of fear. Rather, they are deterrents that slow progress, erode self-confidence, and create confusion in the decision-making processes.

You will discover ways to go over, around, through, or under each trap. When you fall into one, you can find a way out.

I can't imagine anybody avoiding all the traps, and, quite frankly, the effort required to get out of one can lead to remarkable personal growth.

Some natural outcomes of spousal death are not traps at the start, but can become traps quickly if left unaddressed.

Loneliness is the first and foremost example.

The feeling of loneliness is inescapable—most likely to appear early and stay late. Loneliness can manifest itself as simply the emptiness of your home when you walk in expecting to see your spouse in a favorite chair, reading a book, watching television, or involved in a dearly-loved hobby.

Or, loneliness can be complex, as when you try to communicate with the deceased about something that happened at work, or with the kids, or any number of other things you talked about regularly, yet in mid-sentence you remember he or she is no longer there. No matter which way you turn, loneliness becomes your shadow.

Even when you go out to dinner, or a movie, or some other activity with friends, co-workers or family, the diversion usually is short-lived, because at the end of the evening you still come back to the empty home, and loneliness is waiting there for you.

If you have children at home, as I do, they can only fill a portion of the void. Some psychologists say that the depth of our loneliness is tied to the amount of individual identity that existed in the marital rela-tionship. For some the two identities that came together on their wedding day evolved into an almost totally-single identity, with little expressed individuality. The couple did everything together, rarely one without the other, and a noticeable harmony existed in their relation-ship. For others, individuality remained intact. While they had their married life, which might well have been quite strong, they also main-tained a well-defined identity outside the marriage, perhaps related to a profession or a specialized hobby.

You could be thinking that if loneliness is such a natural part of grief, then what can be done about it? Loneliness, as with so many of the barriers we encounter, is a by-product of the disintegration of a desired state of normalcy. As this woman or man who was so important in our lives is taken away, and as we comprehend how we depended on them, loneliness grows rapidly, and continues to grow until we develop and make a transition to a new state of normalcy.

I said earlier that loneliness does not start out as a trap, but can become one quickly if it is not addressed. When loneliness becomes a trap it can and does lead to other very serious traps, such as isolation, substance abuse, and entering into new relationships too soon.

How did I deal with my loneliness? In the beginning, not very well, I must say. I thought that the solution was to go out, meet new people, maybe even start dating. Soon I realized I was getting nowhere, at least nowhere near where I wanted to go. I addressed my loneliness, and all I did was make it worse.

What I realize now is that my first inclinations were based on who I was before I married. I had not yet begun to mold my new identity. Remember in Chapter 2 the question, "Who am I?" My attempt to fill the void of my loneliness caused me to ask the question, and begin an earnest search for the answer. The search helped me identify that my actions were not aligned with my beliefs.

I was telling myself I was one person, but then acting like someone else. To truly address this issue I would have to create my new identity.

Eventually I identified two primary stages to my loneliness.

The first stage dealt with the loneliness generated by the loss of my spouse—the reality that my companion, my friend, my lover, the one who brought a very special meaning to my life, was gone. That loneliness was rooted both in my loss and in my efforts to continue living in that former state of normalcy. That stage of loneliness began to subside as I acknowledged and accepted the reality that the former state could no longer exist.

Please notice that I said began to subside. The loneliness did not, has not, and probably will not go away totally until the start of a new relationship. The level of loneliness diminished, though, to a level I can deal with.

As I began creating the new state of normalcy, the second stage of loneliness joined the scene, based in the basic human need for companionship. A sense of urgency sets in to develop a new, meaningful relationship. The loneliness in this second stage doesn't bear the same degree of hurting, but it was far more scary than the first stage. New relationships can be a trap.

Anger is a second natural outcome that can become a trap. Depending on the circumstances surrounding your spouse's death, your anger might be directed at God, at the deceased, at yourself, at a medical services staff, at the perpetrator (in the case of a violent death), or someone else, anyone.

Anger is normal, and in most cases therapeutic value comes from acknowledging and expressing the anger you feel. Positive value comes when anger leads to a deeper understanding of ourselves and our relationship with the deceased. However, the trap comes when we obsessively blame others for our misfortune, even if the blame is accurate.

While anger never was a dominant behavior for me, some specific instances occurred when I did become angry. Primarily those centered on events with our children that Jada was not able to participate in.

A third natural outcome is **worry**. I am sure that during marriage each of us struggled at times with a host of problems that seemed to have no answer.

Worry is often times the result of those struggles. No one is a stranger to this condition, and worry seems to be human nature. However, when our spouse was alive we at least had a companion with whom we could jointly discuss and attack the situations that arose. Surviving spouses face those struggles alone, and they seem to arise more often. What might have seemed to be an insignificant problem when we were married, today, alone, looks insurmountable. Grief has a way of magnifying everything.

The trap is not imbedded in the normal worries that we face, nor is it learning how to face them alone. The trap is what I call, *the state of perpetual worry*—a condition where every decision is perceived to be a crisis, and the fear of making a wrong decision leads to a state of human inertia. The fear of being wrong leaves one often choosing to do nothing.

Perpetual worry feeds off itself, creating a spiraling effect. Just as success breeds confidence of more success, failure breeds fear of more failure. And since grief clouds judgment and decision-making ability, the failure-breeds-failure syndrome seems more dominant. The resultant worry is all-consuming if allowed to continue unabated.

Reducing worry is a by-product of learning how to make better decisions. Some suggestions for improving decision-making:

1. Identify what is truly most important in your life. Focus attention, time, and energy on what is *essentially* important, not just what seems urgent. While each problem must be addressed, not every problem must be addressed today. Understand the consequences of delaying a decision, but understand as well that deciding to address something today could result in failing to address a more important *immediate* issue.

2. Every problem has alternative solutions. The extremes are do nothing and knee-jerk reaction. The extremes seldom result in the best solution. Take time to evaluate the available alternatives and then make an informed decision.

3. Get help. Someone you know has the ability and the willingness to help you work through the alternatives. The decision must ultimately be yours, but input from others can help you make better decisions.

4. Don't second-guess yourself. If you make a mistake, and, trust me, you will make mistakes, acknowledge them, accept them, learn from them, and then make the necessary course corrections.

Now I want to cover some of the traps I have identified during my journey. Please remember that a trap is anything that becomes a deterrent which slows progress, erodes self-confidence, or impacts ability to make good decisions. Since each individual is different it stands to reason that each is more susceptible to some traps, and less susceptible to others.

Someone Else's Loss is Greater Than Yours

I fell in this trap at least twice. I rationalized ways to minimize the loss. When I learned the news of some tragedy in the world, such as how an entire family was lost in an accident or natural disaster, I found myself thinking how fortunate I was to not have to deal with what those survivors were enduring. Even hearing about the death of a child caused me to rationalize that at least it wasn't one of my own children.

Basically, my inner voice said that I shouldn't feel too bad, it could have been worse. By trying to minimize the loss I delayed acknowledgement of just how significant my personal loss was. Of course it could have been worse, but that in no way reduces its impact. All spousal death is a great loss to the surviving spouse.

Another element of this trap that I encountered stemmed from the question, "Which is worse, a sudden death due to an accident or violent event, or a death resulting from a lingering illness or disease?" For some time I rationalized that a sudden death would be far more painful. It seemed to me that those of us who lost our spouse after an extended illness at least had the opportunity to experience some form of reconciliation, some opportunity to say goodbye.

What I came to realize was that all death is sudden. Even when death is imminent, we hold out for a miracle. Therefore, when the death occurs most of us experience shock that the one we loved is gone. The shock, while different perhaps, is nonetheless traumatic to the individual.

In dealing with cancer you know that death is a possibility. So why do I consider Jada's death sudden? Because throughout her treatment we chose to be almost blindly optimistic even though we knew death was a possibility. Our belief was that we should maintain a steady stream of positive energy and avoid the negative energy associated with thoughts of death.

By the time we got to Tulsa she was so sick we were unable, or unwilling, to recognize and acknowledge what was about to happen. On the 10th day after our arrival she was placed in intensive care, and before that night was over a respirator was required to sustain her life. Neither of us could communicate—she because of heavy sedation, me because of the numbness of the situation. Her slide toward death was so rapid that we had no time to say goodbye, to effect any type of personal reconciliation.

Guilt

Not only did I fall in this trap, I stayed in it for quite awhile. What do we have to feel guilty about? Maybe we feel we should have pushed the deceased to get medical help sooner. Maybe we feel we should have been more understanding. Maybe the marriage had not been doing so well. Maybe we said that tomorrow we could make up for the little hurts we had caused over the years, but tomorrow never came. Maybe guilt prevails because your spouse is gone, and you are still alive. Countless reasons exist for feeling guilty.

In Chapter 5 I referred to one form of guilt with which I dealt over concern with whether or not I was healing too quickly, too easily, and if this was in some way disrespectful to Jada's memory. The second form of guilt dealt not with the present, but with the past. At the time I was dealing with my loss more on an intellectual basis, rather than emotionally.

I discovered that this strong sense of guilt arose over the problems I had caused in our marriage, problems which had been significant during the three years preceding her diagnosis. I compounded the problem since I knew Jada had felt guilt also, but wasn't here to deal with it, so I felt compelled to take on her guilt as well as my own. It sounds silly now, but it was very real. The feeling of guilt was so strong that it dominated my life for more than a month. Fortunately a good friend encouraged me to seek counseling, which I did. The counselor helped me identify the guilt issues, and suggested some techniques to resolve them. It was truly a major step in my journey. We cover professional counseling in Chapter 8.

The key to overcoming guilt is forgiveness. Not just asking forgiveness from your spouse, but asking for self-forgiveness. We must accept that if the deceased were here with us, and we asked their forgiveness they would lovingly give it. Also, we must lovingly forgive the deceased for her or his failures. This ritualistic event has a cleansing effect that brought harmony out of discord for me.

Obsessive/Compulsive Behavior

I want to be very careful with this topic. Obsessive/compulsive behavior can be a psychological disorder best treated professionally. It is not my intention to address that extreme level of the behavior.

As I have said repeatedly in previous chapters the emotional pain associated with the death of a spouse can be severe. My experience indicates that it hurt far worse during idle time, when I was not occupied with some activity. I found that if I kept busy the pain left, at least for a little while. There is nothing wrong with trying to get away from the pain, and if being active works for you, then I would encourage you to stay active.

How does this become a trap? It becomes obsessive/compulsive behavior when it is used continuously to avoid the source of your emotional pain, the death of your spouse. By immersing yourself in work, community service, church, and family, you can neglect the strong need to grieve properly and experience the healing power of the grief process. In the throes of emotional pain a strong tendency creeps up often to look for ways to get away from it.

The activities I mentioned are logical choices because they are such accepted practices. Used properly the acceptable activities can be excellent support tools for your journey. Used constantly to avoid facing the challenges of grieving, they can become barriers to your progress.

When our spouse dies we must assume new roles, particularly if there are still children in the home. Some of us, myself included, will become trapped in developing this new role identity. I felt I had to do everything she would have done, and I had to do it well. It was nothing to stay up late to clean the house, wash clothes, or perform other household duties.

I became obsessed with doing it all, and became angry at myself when I did not meet my expectations. This behavior, while perhaps admirable on the surface, hurt both me and my children. Being a good housekeeper was not a part of dealing with my grief; conversely, becoming Mr. Mom was a deterrent to dealing with my grief. I focused on things that weren't most important in my life, taking away from the balance I was trying to achieve. Most of all, my ability to focus on my grief waned. At times I still struggle with this, but I am now able to recognize when I have lost the desired balance, and to make the necessary corrections.

Single Parenting

Obviously this trap will not apply to everyone, but for those who lose their spouse while young children still live in the home, they present one of the greatest challenges you will face. Our children Charlie, Chris, and Chad, were ages 16, 11, and 7 when their mother died. During our marriage Jada had never worked outside the home, so she was the most visible parent in the eyes of our children. I learned quickly after her death that I had much to learn about parenting, and it involved far more effort than I had realized.

The demands on a single parent, trying to work, and trying to deal with my grief all at the same time, made me feel like a rat trapped in a maze. No matter which direction I took I seemed to always end up back at the same spot, never finding the elusive prize.

Even on those rare occasions when I achieved a victory, the satisfaction was fleeting, as I was unable to either repeat the steps or sustain the gains. Further complicating matters, myriad new issues entered into the equation—non-issues when there were two of us, such as child care before and after school.

Having just lost my spouse caused me to be fearful that something might happen to one of the kids, which resulted in a potentially suffocating over-protectiveness. Each child wanted and needed something different, which confounded me even more. Charlie wanted the freedom to spread his wings. Chris, who has Attention Deficit Disorder, needed my encouragement. And Chad, who as the youngest was truly his mother's boy, needed my reassurance.

For my part I wanted to be the perfect parent, thinking I could to do it all and do it right every time. Put it all together, shake well, and you have a bomb waiting to go off! Fortunately no bombs ever truly went off, and while I could share many stories about the challenges of single parenting, there is one which I believe enabled me to make a major transition as a parent and a person.

The story began with the start of the first school year after Jada's death. As usual Chris struggled early with maintaining focus in the classroom, due primarily to Attention Deficit Disorder. His grades were like a yo-yo. I tried to be encouraging, but he felt I was always angry and threatening to punish him.

By the second semester his grades and his behavior were wildly erratic. When report cards came out at the end of the fourth grading period his marks were bad. I lost my temper, verbally berated him, and threatened that he would lose every privilege known to mankind if he didn't get his act together and show improvement. It was not a very pretty sight, nor something I am proud of. I'm not sure why I thought this was going to help the situation, but I'm sure I rationalized something.

Approximately three weeks later I arrived home from work one evening and found a note on the kitchen table from Chris. Basically it said that he had received his interim grades for the fifth six- week period and they were bad. Then he wrote that everything was his fault and I should punish him for doing so poorly. The tone of the note was that he was a bad person who should be punished. Tears came to my eyes immediately, and I said to myself, "My God, what have I done?" I had wanted to help my son with his problem, but all I succeeded in doing was further damaging his self-esteem.

I couldn't help him change until I helped myself change. I vowed to get him whatever help he needed and to provide him with encouragement, support, and, yes, an appropriate level and type of discipline. But never again would I subject him to verbal abuse.

While there have been no miracles here—Chris still struggles to maintain focus—significant changes have taken place in the way we deal with the struggles. I have traded in my typical fly-off-the-handle, knee-jerk reaction for a more patient, listening and understanding approach. Stephen Covey, author of the *Seven Habits of Highly Effective People*, says that this method, "seeks first to understand, rather than be understood."

The approach is not perfect, nor am I perfect in executing it, but the positive influence is clear on how we deal with the multitude of problems that arise. The realizations that stem from this example are that I am not now, nor will I ever be a perfect parent, and by the same token my children are not going to be perfect either; mistakes are OK, and that I must be as willing to forgive myself for my shortcomings as I am willing to forgive others for theirs.

FOOTNOTE on Dealing with Children's Grief

Children's grief is associated with the trap of single parenting. Minor children experience a world turned upside-down by the death of a parent. Typically, surviving parents do not discuss death with children, or, when they do, the explanation frequently extends beyond the child's comprehension. That makes sense, because in many ways the loss of a spouse is beyond the surviving spouse's comprehension.

Psychologists I talked with indicate that children grieve differently from adults. Children tend to process grief in small chunks over a period of years, whereas adults tend to become consumed immediately with all aspects of their grief.

The level of a child's demonstrated grief will depend in part on two factors:

1. The depth of the relationship between the deceased parent and the child, and

2. The ability of the surviving parent and other adults in the child's support circle to encourage open expressions of grief.

Even though I was consumed by my own grief I knew it was essential to create an environment right away in which our children could feel comfortable in asking questions about their mother's death.

One evening during the week after Jada's funeral, as part of a homework assignment Chad, the youngest, read a story to me. After finishing, he said, "I wish mom could have heard me read that story. She always liked to hear me read." As I wept, I told him that his mother probably was listening the whole time, and in all likelihood she was sitting on the back of our chair smiling at every word he read. This reassured him that although her physical presence was gone, his mother's spiritual presence would always remain with him.

In the months that followed I encouraged our children to talk about their mother whenever they felt the need; to cry when they felt like crying, and to ask any question they wanted an answer to. Many times we cried together as we discussed how much we missed Jada. Yet, we spent much more time remembering fondly the fun times we shared as a family.

Today neither the questions nor the tears come as often, but when they do, they still receive the same level of importance as during those first difficult months. I believe this has had a significant impact on the children's recovery, and subsequently, has given them the ability to accept and love the new mother they have been sent (see Epilogue).

Substance Abuse

From the moment of a spouse's death emotional pain becomes a constant companion. The level of pain varies, but even in moments devoid of all pain, very little comfort is forthcoming because of the anticipation of more right around the corner. In seeking relief from emotional pain, many persons resort to the use of alcohol or medication to help get over the rough spots. Guided by a physician, and using common sense, the use of prescription medicine or alcohol poses little threat. However, at times when the pain mounts to a point of clouding judgment, the stage is set for misuse or abuse.

Men are more apt to misuse alcohol, while women are more likely to misuse sedatives. Misuse can cause dependency on these substances to make the pain go away, even when the evidence is clear that the relief is only temporary. Anyone falling into this trap should seek qualified medical help as soon as possible to get back on the right track.

New relationships

At an appropriate time, rightfully and naturally, many surviving spouses will want to build new primary relationships. The catch phrase here is appropriate time. According to psychologists you should wait a minimum of one year, and preferably two years or more before entering into a new relationship.

The rationale suggests that during the first year after the death of a spouse the survivor confronts so many new and challenging elements that he or she is ill-prepared to take on the challenges of a new relationship. The grief process strips an individual of emotional defenses, leaving the raw edges exposed, a matter for immediate concern. This exposure places the person at risk for additional emotional distress in the attempt to balance grieving for the deceased with developing a new relationship.

Judgment and decision-making ability generally leave a lot to be desired during grief recovery, which complicates the dynamics of a relationship. Unfortunately I didn't know anything about this during my first year, so I had to find out the hard way.

Long before Jada died, even long before she was diagnosed, she asked me if I would remarry, should anything ever happen to her. I remember my puzzlement with the question. I figured the question was one that has no right answer, and if you don't choose your answer carefully you end up in the doghouse.

So I made a joke of it, saying, "Heck, no, why would I want to do this again?" If there was a right answer, that definitely wasn't it. The look on her face told me that instantly. Rebuked, Jada responded, "Well, thanks a lot, that really speaks well of the value I've added to your life."

That episode stuck with me throughout our years together. What she was looking for was some assurance that she had brought me happiness in our marriage. Therefore upon her death I rationalized that one of the greatest tributes I could pay her was to develop a new relationship that resulted in my remarrying. A side note to this was the way our younger children missed having the special touch that only a mother (biological or otherwise) can provide.

This became a trap for me, not because I had a desire to re-marry, for I truly believed that the married state was necessary for me to be happy, but because of the timing of trying to move toward that state. I attempted to develop a relationship about eight months after Jada's death. Fortunately the woman involved was a lot smarter than I, and she knew that I was rushing things. As a result the downside was my badly-bruised ego. The upside was a valuable lesson from a very special person to whom I will always be grateful. I know now that I could have been hurt badly by the experience, and I urge you to proceed cautiously in this area.

Several months ago I heard a psychologist tell the story of a recently widowed individual he was counseling who, shortly after his spouse's death, entered into a relationship that resulted in marriage. In less than a year this person was consulting the psychologist again—for divorce counseling. Now, rather than the one emotional trauma, he had two.

Exercising patience in this area is not easy, and I am sure cases exist where new relationships have worked well. However, in honesty, surely we can agree that the long-term risks are far greater than any short-term benefits to be derived.

Isolation

Upon the death of a spouse, highly supportive family members and friends show up everywhere. I welcomed and needed their support, as I certainly was not operating at peak capability to handle many of the tasks at hand. Sometimes family or friends stay with the surviving spouse up to several weeks, making sure that needs are met.

At some point, however, they return to their families and get on with their lives. Often they maintain contact, but gradually that diminishes, also, or certainly the content of the contact changes.

This natural event, coupled with the probable onset of loneliness, can drive us to become isolated from much of the outside world. Most instances of isolation are unintentional, and from what I have seen, heard, and experienced typically come from not knowing how to deal with the the suffering of emotional pain and uncertainty.

Isolation can take several forms. In the extreme, we sit in our homes with the shades drawn, lights down low, seeing no one, and venturing outside only when absolutely necessary. We believe that our pain is so great that we can't possibly relate to or interact with anyone, so we basically lock ourselves away from the rest of the world.

In another form, we rationalize our isolation because of perceived responsibilities to our children. Obviously, a single parent with young children takes on new responsibilities that can't be ignored. However, an obsessive behavior can set in for taking care of their every need without ever considering any of your own personal needs. An unintended outcome of this behavior is isolation from others by using parental responsibilities as an excuse for not accepting invitations to any of a number of interactive events.

A third form of isolation occurs during a desire for interaction, but the individual is uncertain how to proceed. He or she waits for someone else to issue a dinner invitation, or offers to go shopping, or a social event, etc., and when those invitations don't come the thought can prevail that friends have forgotten about them. Two conditions bring this on.

1. Either friends (most of whom have never experienced what we are going through) don't understand the surviving spouse's needs or how they can help, or

2. In many cases when asked, "How are you doing?" or when help is offered, the surviving spouse responds with comments like, "I'm doing as well as I can expect," or "I can't think of anything I need."

That continued response makes it extremely difficult for others to provide anything more than basic support. Such support generally is received in a very narrow scope, such as at work or church, not necessarily when needed the most. Not because no one wants to help, rather because they don't know what or when to give. The key is to ask for what you want or need.

Often, a complicating factor stems from awkwardness over having a circle of friends composed only of other married couples. You might have been part of a group of couples who dined together, or went on trips together, and with the death of your spouse those group relationships changed. You might find it too painful to continue doing things with the group. Maybe you feel like a fifth wheel, that you don't belong. The other members of the group, grieving in their own way, feel equally awkward—afraid that including you in their plans will place you in emotionally difficult situations. When you find yourself excluded you could begin to believe that you have been deserted.

A couple of suggestions are in order here:

1. Tell the most talkative person among your group that you are now ready to be included in group activities. Rest assured this will get around to the other group members.

2. Invite the group to your house for the evening.

Isolation is one of the most dangerous traps – a leading cause of depression among surviving spouses. You can best avoid isolation through involvement in activities such as work, community service, or church. Which activity you choose is not nearly as important as the fact that you choose an activity of some type.

If, on your journey to living again, you encounter other traps (the next chapter deals with several smaller ones) the same fundamental principles will apply. Find a way to surmount them.

A final note of caution: these traps have a tendency to appear, disappear, and reappear throughout the journey. You might avoid a trap once, only to fall into it later. You can even fall into two or more traps at the same time. Also, the longer you stay mired in a trap the greater the probability that a more damaging trap will appear, making it that much more difficult to get out.

Hope is brightest when it dawns from our fears.

—Walter Scott

Chapter 7
Smaller Traps

Originally I had planned to treat the subject of traps as one complete topic. However, as I progressed through the outline I realized that two types of traps exist—the big ones covered in Chapter 6, and the smaller ones I will cover now.

Small traps essentially consist of day-to-day nuisances that cause you to stumble, such as who is going to do the dishes or the laundry, go grocery shopping, or carpool the kids? While they do not literally block progress, they do slow it down. These traps become little more than an aggravation or source of frustration—niggling, perhaps, but nonetheless nettlesome.

The small traps tend to correlate to the surviving spouse's gender and age. Much of the impact of these traps depends on the role definition that existed in the marriage, and how responsibilities were shared or not shared. Regardless of how capable each of us is, our spouse performed numerous tasks 100 percent of the time. Because he or she did them does not mean that you and I are incapable of doing them, only that we either never have or have not in a long time.

Some typical, specific examples:

For men

1. Primary child care.

2. Making appointments for the doctor or dentist.

3. Parent/teacher meetings.

4. Dealing with minor medical crises (first aid).

5. Preparing/eating healthy meals.

6. Housekeeping/laundry.

7. Onset of puberty for a daughter.

8. Buying clothes.

9. Grocery shopping.

10. Shopping for school supplies.

For women

1. Car care.

2. Painting, minor plumbing, or home repair projects.

3. Electrical problems.

4. Filling your car up with gas.

5. Finances.

6. Tax return preparation.

7. Yardwork.

8. Seasonal maintenance of lawn care equipment.

9. Entertaining couples.

10. Assembling purchases, i.e. lawnmowers, bicycles.

The lists could go on and on, and certainly they will vary in different households and relationships, but I'm sure you get the point. I had always thought of myself as very domesticated. I frequently cooked, washed dishes, loaded and folded laundry, shopped for groceries, the works.

However, with Jada gone, I quickly realized that I had only been a helper. When there were two of us to share the responsibilities the tasks seemed relatively simple. When they all fell on my shoulders I realized how much is involved, and how many little things must be done that I was not even aware of. The harsh reality of becoming a single parent was eye-opening, as well.

During those first few, difficult months after your spouse is gone, with the addition of new responsibilities, or at least newly-defined, well … many times you just do not have enough hours in the day to get done all that you believe you need to have done. Even if there were enough hours, would you have enough energy? Doubtful.

Not only is the tendency strong to want to do everything, but to expect to do it well, if not perfect. The frustration that builds can lead to serious doubt about your capability, and to lower self-esteem—at a time when they have already taken a beating. Like a dog chasing its tail, you run yourself ragged in circles, never quite reaching the objective.

Another side of this equation reveals situations in which surviving spouses literally refuse to even try to take on new responsibilities, many times thinking they can't do it. There is an old saying that "can't never could."

In your recovery journey, can't is not an option. While many of the new tasks seem unpleasant and daunting, and you might feel quite awkward at first, you will become better at them as you move forward, provided you make the attempt.

And remember, we're not talking about the proverbial old college try here; we're talking about a commitment to living again. That involves a total commitment to life style renewal and to restructuring your thinking and your behavior, which in turn strengthens your feelings and well-being, as well as other persons around you.

The key for me was to seek balance between the roles I was playing. I prioritized and focused on those things that were truly important, and kept firmly in mind that while it might seem that everything must get done, not everything must get done today. It has not been easy to achieve this balance, and many days have an impossible feel to them.

On those days I endeavor to accept them as reality and strive to be more balanced the next day.

When you look at how many traps dot the path of this challenging journey, is there any wonder why so often we struggle? Have faith, for just as there are traps that threaten to keep you from your goal, you have an array of personal power tools to help you break out of the traps and keep you moving forward toward your goals.

Let us realize that what happens around us is largely outside of our control, but that the way we choose to react to it is inside of our control.

—Anonymous

Chapter 8
Tools

As we have said repeatedly, the goal of living again is to create a new state of normalcy. The journey has no specified length, and the path is fraught with potential traps. Fortunately, an array of powerful tools is available with which to repair and build. The tool chest is full.

A tool is anything that enables insight and perspective, the main ingredients necessary to stay on course. Tools allow you to see and avoid traps, to get out of traps you have fallen into, or to keep you marching on track when you are tired, frustrated, and scared. Like the traps, the tools are interrelated; they support and strengthen each other, and you. They fall into four categories:

❖ Spiritual self.

❖ Emotional self.

❖ Intellectual self.

❖ Physical self.

Even before our spouses died each surviving spouse possessed at least some level of developed capability to use every tool. Expanding that capability and using the tools throughout the grief journey is of utmost importance. Each interrelated tool has depth and breadth.

Tools of the Spiritual Self

The tools of the spiritual self are not limited to Christians. Every culture in our world has some organized religious institution(s), and while they take different forms they contain many similarities. Therefore, while discussion here focuses on a Christian perspective, I am confident that the content applies in the context of any other religion or spiritual bent.

The development of the spiritual self usually begins at a very early age. Any of several paths lead many people into a lifetime of active spiritual growth and practice of a faith in traditional religious institutions, i.e., the organized church.

For some this development starts out strong, but over the years they wandered away from active participation. Others search for meaning outside of traditional religious institutions, even though holding to a fundamental belief in a supreme being, often referred to as a Higher Power.

Still others spend a lifetime questioning the very existence of their spiritual self. And some individuals never received early exposure to any faith system or practice.

Regardless of which path you find yourself on, death has a uniquely spiritual significance for the overwhelming majority.

The death of a spouse causes many of us to question God's judgment, to question how much He loves us, to question the power of prayer, or to question our faith. We become angry with God for taking away this person we loved so dearly and planned to spend a longer life with.

We might even wonder if He is punishing us for past sins. These reactions are neither uncommon, nor unexpected. I believe that God understands these reactions, and provides us with responses if we use the spiritual tools at hand.

While I want to avoid a theological debate, I believe some commonly held spiritual truths serve as good reminders here:

1. There is one true God, although He may be called by many names.

2. He has a plan for our lives, which includes when we are to be called home to our reward.

3. Death affects only the body; the spirit lives on eternally.

4. Where and how we spend eternity depends on how we conduct ourselves in this life.

5. God grants a spiritual strength that enables us to meet all challenges we face.

6. God is always with us, walking beside us in our joyful times, carrying us in our times of greatest need.

Many of us have used the spiritual tools of prayer, scripture study, reflection, and active participation in church to varying degrees throughout our personal and spiritual development. The loss of a spouse causes us to look at the use of those tools in a different light.

One final note on spiritual tools: Humans have a strong tendency to want to see before we believe; with spiritual tools we must first believe, then we will see.

Prayer

What is your prayer life like? What do you say or ask for when you talk to God? How does God talk to you?

Prayer is a channel of communication to God. It requires only that we approach God with reverence, with sincerity, with a penitent heart - aloud, or in silence; in church, in the privacy of home, lying in bed, or while driving a car.

Frankly, I believe God is more concerned with the substance and sincerity of prayers than the formalities.

Prayer speaks directly to God and asks Him for what we need - for forgiveness, for strength, for courage, for wisdom, for understanding, for patience, for the sick, for our dearly departed loved ones, for emotional and spiritual healing.

Prayer also prepares your heart to receive God's answer. Although God speaks to us whether we have an active prayer life or not, I am not sure how well we can hear him without prayer as an integral part of our lives.

Throughout Jada's treatment my prayer life increased significantly. I always asked for God's healing hand to be placed on her. I also asked that God's will be done, and if it was His will that she be taken from us I asked that she be spared the pain and suffering of an extended illness. I believe my prayers were answered.

Her purpose in this life was finished, so the miracle of physical healing was not an option. She was, however, spared the pain and suffering that so often accompanies cancer, and for that I am truly grateful.

God continues to answer my prayers by giving me the strength to handle the challenges I encounter, the wisdom to seek and understand His plan for my life, and the courage to follow His plan. When I stumble - and I do stumble all too frequently - I can usually identify the reason as a failure in my prayer life.

Bible Study

As prayer establishes communication with God, scripture study provides vivid examples of how God demonstrates His love to those who believe and trust in Him. Scripture illuminates the path to follow in demonstrating our love for Him. Throughout scripture, constant references appear about how God strengthens our spirit even in the face of seemingly insurmountable obstacles.

If you doubt this then I encourage you to read the Book of Job. The Psalms can provide comfort in your most troubled times. Paul's letters to the early churches (e.g., Corinthians I and II) provide examples of how to keep yourself on the right track for achieving your goal.

Yet as good as each of these is, nothing comes close to the gospels of Matthew, Mark, Luke, and John. Studying, understanding, and then following the example of Jesus Christ leads to the close, personal relationship with God that is essential to living again.

Active Participation

Active participation is an expression of the need of people with similar beliefs to worship together in a declaration of faith, conviction, and desire to grow in God's love. Regardless of your affiliation with a traditional church denomination or otherwise, or even if you worship in a non-denominational sector, you will find a special strength through regular attendance and participation in your worship services.

If you are not affiliated with a church or worship group, I encourage you to seek and associate with a group that can meet your needs for spiritual growth and support. Regular participation provides the strength necessary for your journey.

Be aware of some probable emotional issues:

1. If you and the deceased attended services together regularly, and typically sat in the same place every week, expect to sense a feeling of loneliness or emptiness when you see his or her empty seat.

2. If the funeral services took place in the church you regularly attend then you might be confronted with the visual image of the casket, the flowers, etc. I was amazed at how vivid those images were, and to this day I still see them periodically.

3. If the music at the funeral service featured regular selections from your weekly services, prepare yourself for an emotional surge whenever you hear the songs. I have no doubt that for the rest of my life I will tear up every time I hear "On Eagle's Wings" and "Be Not Afraid."

I probably cry more at church than anywhere else, but I've decided that is okay. The benefits of active participation, and from confronting the emotional memories far outweigh any negatives.

Reflection

This tool develops the breadth and depth of what we learn through prayer and scripture study. Reflection brings about application of the learning, and creates substantive change by using God's gifts. God reveals many things through prayer and scripture about healing, gaining inner strength, His plan, and more. But knowing these things is of limited value if we don't use that knowledge. Reflection is not limited to the spiritual tools, and can be put to use through all the tool groups.

So what is reflection? Simply thinking about things? Simply seeking understanding? Finding meaning? Reflection is all this, and more. Reflection is looking in a mirror at the soul, and seeing where we are and who we are; where we were and who we were, and comparing the images with where we want to be and who we want to be.

Reflection develops perspective, clarity, and definition in understanding God's plan for us. Good choices come from reflection, enabling forward progress toward the goal, measurement of that progress, and, yes, reflection even fosters understanding of our bad choices.

Reflection must take place on two levels to be most effective – past to present, and present to future. In the first level we examine how far we have come. How well did we live up to what we said we wanted to accomplish in our previous reflection? What did we learn about ourselves? Were we able to sustain previous gains? (Sometimes it is easier to achieve something than to hold on to it.)

In the second level we track where we are on the path to goal achievement, what the next steps involve, and verify understanding of the goal. This is easier than it might sound. When reflecting, take some general precautions:

1. Reflection will uncover both successes and failures. Commonly we ignore what we did well and focus only on what we did poorly. I encourage you to pat yourself on the back continually for your successes. You cannot beat yourself up for your failures. When you make a mistake acknowledge it, accept it, and learn from it.

2. Although goal-setting can be useful, proceed with caution. Set goals that meet the criteria of realistic and achievable. Remain open to suggestions, but disallow anybody from setting goals for you. Initially, you focus on making it through the next day, the next week, so make only goals that fit your current needs, and only within your control. Long-term goals become appropriate at some point, but not at the outset.

3. The loss of your spouse has an effect like a natural disaster might have on your home, such as a fire. In rebuilding a destroyed home we start with the foundation, followed by the framework, then the exterior walls, then the roof, and so on until completion. Each step depends on the previous steps, and if the roof goes on before its time, it will collapse. This holds true in rebuilding lives as well. A solid foundation provides the strength and stability necessary to weather the future, the inevitable. Reflection determines the proper order for rebuilding a life.

Developing the ability to use, and then putting to use the spiritual tools provides two essential elements of your journey – healing the wounds of grief, and searching for and understanding God's plan for your life. In light of the healing power of the spiritual tools, I would be remiss not to discuss the spiritual tools in the context of God's plan.

For years most of us have been living God's plan, albeit with varying degrees of success. The marriage partner was part of that plan. But how that changed when that spouse died, creating a state of uncertainty, a state of fear, a state of doubt. Searching for and finding the next part of God's plan for you is a critical step in the process of truly living again.

Start the search for the next stage of God's plan in your life with three truths:

1. God has a total plan for your life, which He reveals according to His timetable. The deceased spouse was a part of that plan.

2. God endows you with talents or gifts for use in following His plan. We demonstrate our love for God when we use our talents for His glory.

3. The next part of God's plan for you might differ totally from the last part. To illustrate, this is how cognizance in these areas led me to write this book.

I never planned to be a writer, let alone write this particular book. My entire business career had been spent working in management positions for three different manufacturing companies. I developed and used my talents to move up the ladder, ultimately receiving a promotion to Plant Manager about a month before Jada's diagnosis.

In retrospect, I'd say I used my talents more for my glory than for God's. The demands of the new position, coupled with the demands of being a caretaker, husband, and father took a toll over the next 20 months. Around the time of Jada's death my employer, who had been very understanding about my difficulties, recognized that the company needed to move forward, and that I needed to focus my attention on things more important than work. We agreed that I would move out of the Plant Manager role, and work instead on a variety of business-related projects, until I was ready for a new permanent assignment.

Over the course of the next several months the business went through major changes, and evidence mounted that any future, permanent assignments I might receive in that company probably would require relocation of my family. At that point I really began searching for what

Living Again

God's plan for me was.

Through prayer and reflection He began to lead me to the answer. I say began to lead me because the first answers were more along the lines of what his plan was not.

The first answer to my prayerful search came when I realized that staying with the organization would require relocation further away from my extended family, away from my base of support. I concluded that this would not be in the best interest of my children, or me, and therefore decided that any assignment that would require me to move further away would not be acceptable.

This decision assured that I would not remain with my employer much longer, and in fact I was told during mid-summer that I would be laid off by the end of the year.

With that issue resolved, where do I go next?

As I continued to search for God's plan, two alternatives became clear: continue similar work for a different company, or start my own business. Another variable was staying in Memphis or moving back to Alabama where I would be closer to my family. The option of moving back to Alabama became more appealing when my father died while these decisions pressed on my mind.

As my last day of work drew near I was as confused as ever, and the confusion heightened with the idea of a new alternative – writing a book about the grief process.

I prayed and reflected, prayed and reflected, and then prayed and reflected some more. Every time I weighed the options this idea of writing a book generated more and more inner peace. I resisted. My faith was not strong enough.

Then at the suggestion of my sister-in-law I read the Book of Jonah, which made me realize how futile it was to resist God. I still wasn't convinced fully, so I prayed and reflected some more. Finally, I said, "God, if this is how you want to use my talents then I will trust you to give me the words, to give me the understanding, to give me the strength to follow your plan."

The inner peace this decision created within me is difficult to describe, but wonderful to live. God has been with me, and guided me throughout the exercise of writing this book. As I have periodically struggled to know what to write, or how to write it, He has opened my heart and mind to His plan.

Some will label this purely coincidence, and they certainly are entitled to their opinions. I only know where I was a year ago, and the journey I have gone through to get the inner peace I have today. I know that if I will continue to search, God will continue to reveal His plan to me.

The spiritual tools are the foundation of the healing process. The ability to use them begins with faith. And whether your faith is great or small it will begin to grow and continue to grow through the frequent and sincere use of *prayer, scripture study, active participation, and reflection.*

Tools of the emotional self

To say that the death of your spouse, and the subsequent grief process, is an emotionally-charged situation is an understatement of huge proportions. The emotional pain is borne out of the disintegration of a desired state of normalcy. What you depended on for strength, support, comfort, and love has been stripped away. Doubt, loneliness, and fear remain.

You might have thought of yourself as highly independent, but how quickly you discover how interdependent you were with your husband or wife. Repairing the damage to the emotional self can be a long and frustrating process, and at times the process tests your will to survive.

The tools of the emotional self have great power to help you repair the damage. These tools will help immensely: *crying, family and friends, counseling, support groups, journal writing, and humor.*

Crying

I am amazed at how many people have the notion that once the funeral is over the tears should dry up. How absurd! Crying is an emotional outlet that relieves pent up emotions. In the early stages of grief emotions usually build so rapidly that they must be released several times a day. The frequency and intensity of the release are magnified in the early stages.

The frequency and intensity wane as the grief journey continues, but the need to release emotions by crying remains. Remember, there is no time line to the grief process, and therefore, there is no timeline to the use of expressions of grief.

*** A Special Note for Men ***

Somehow our society has developed a notion that it is not "manly" for men to cry. Get over that, and get over it now, or the emotions that build up will either eat you alive or you will explode – that is, the emotions will come spilling out in ways that are detrimental to your emotional repair.

Never underestimate the therapeutic value of crying, and definitely crying should not be limited to only the early stages of the grief process. Crying is not a sign of weakness; indeed, crying is a sign of strength. Cry now, and cry often.

Family and Friends

Throughout history family has provided the primary support for survivors. This particularly held true when as an agrarian society we lived mostly in extended family groups.

However, the industrial revolution moved masses of people out of their agricultural heritage. This trend, coupled with increased mobility, caused physical and emotional separation from biological families. The role of the extended family was replaced by a network of friends. Both groups have a distinct place in the grief process.

The need for the support of families and friends becomes most evident immediately surrounding the loss of your spouse. However, given the length of the grief process, their continued presence and support is an essential element of healing. No matter how much family and friends love us, all of them will not be able to provide the type of support we need. Some are not inclined to be as visibly supportive as others.

Learning how to ask for and use their help often is difficult and sometimes frustrating for both you and them. As I mentioned in Chapter 6, the problem often centers on the willingness to ask for help, and from our supporters not knowing what we need and how to provide it. Hence, the trap of isolation.

In most cases, those offering support, or whom you will seek for support, have not been through the experience of losing a spouse. Therefore, they generally lack understanding about the road you are travelling. All the more reason that you must ask for what you need.

I know, I know – you don't want to impose, or become a burden to family and friends. That premise causes you either not to ask for help, or to turn down help when it is offered. Letting others help us serves a twofold purpose. Obviously you benefit from the support, but just as importantly, allowing others to give adds value to their lives, too. Of course you should never take advantage of the kindness and generosity of others, but neither should you prevent them from feeling the positive energy generated by helping.

Support from family and friends usually is characterized as either physical or emotional. Physical support comes from helping with household duties such as cleaning, cooking, child care, yard work, repairs, or perhaps even assistance in settling the estate of the deceased.

Emotional support might comprise providing a shoulder to cry on, listening as you pour out your feelings, or advising you on how to handle a particular issue. While it might be nice to have an abundance of supporters, quantity is not as important as depth of quality.

I believe it is important to have at least one person as special friend – anyone whom you trust with your innermost thoughts, someone who knows you and your situation, who loves you unconditionally, who will listen non-judgmentally, and who can offer help as you proceed on your journey. I can't emphasize enough the high value of this special relationship.

Professional Counseling

I had always been one who scoffed at the thought of going to any type of counseling. Just the thought of paying someone to listen to my problems and to tell me I should do this or that to solve them made me somewhat angry. I believed I *could* solve, and *should* solve any problems that might come my way.

How wrong I was. Professional counseling might not be appropriate for every situation, but most of us at one time or another during our journey can benefit greatly from the help of a professionally trained counselor.

Obviously, individuals trapped in depression or substance abuse have an urgent need for counseling and treatment. More commonly, the need arises out of getting stuck in a trap (review Chapters 6 and 7), when, try as you might, you find no way out. The longer you stay in the trap, the greater the probability that you cannot get out by yourself.

Professional counselors don't solve problems, they guide you to the answers and self-help. The solutions remain in your behavior. The more open you are with the counselor the better assessment he or she can make about the root cause of your problem. These professionals have a unique way of probing with questions that cause you to look deeply for answers, which can lead to a valuable discovery about yourself. The amount of counseling you require depends on the type of problem, its depth, and your willingness and ability to discuss it openly.

I recall that about six months into the grief process I noticed that I was not getting better and was regressing. After struggling with that for a while, finally, at the suggestion of a friend, I sought help through my Employee Assistance Program (EAP) at work. (Many companies have an EAP benefit, and often the employee is not aware of it. Check with your human resources director.) The counseling I received dispelled any previous doubts I harbored. During our first session the counselor helped me identify that I was dealing with some unresolved guilt over problems in my marriage that I took full responsibility for. This was compounded by my taking on Jada's guilt, which I knew she had felt, but was no longer here to bear.

In a second session we delved deeper into the guilt issue, and into my obsessive tendencies. I received some ideas on how to let go of my guilt through self-forgiveness, and to focus on what was truly important. I am happy to say that this enabled me to get out of the trap and move forward.

Support Groups

I have mentioned several times that most of the people we come in contact with, including family and friends, have limited understanding of what it means to lose a spouse. They are sympathetic and empathetic, but they have no frame of reference for understanding. This particularly rings true at the beginning of the journey through the grief process. This results in some of the gaps that exist in our healing.

Support groups fill in many of those gaps. Something very special comes from sharing with a group of people, all of whom are, or have been, exactly where you are. They have personal knowledge of how you feel. They have personal knowledge of the journey you are undertaking. They have been through the same struggles. They have had the same fears. They have fought the battles and won, and therefore can share with you a special perspective of the journey.

Tools

Support groups come in all shapes and sizes, sponsored by churches, hospitals, other organizations, and some by individuals. Search out one that best fits your personality, your likes and dislikes; I am confident you will find a group which fits well. I consider myself extremely fortunate to be part of a group that provided me with genuine caring and support, and helped me learn about the journey. I have seen myself grow tremendously during my association with this group.

Initially I was a taker, in that I didn't offer a lot but took what others had to offer. As time passed I learned to be a giver and a taker. I still learn much, but I also share what I have learned with others.

Some people feel the need to be in support groups for only a short time, others feel the need to participate much longer. I recommend that you participate for as long as the group participation meets three needs:

1. You are continuing to learn new ways to help you on your journey. This can take several years. You might hear something today, but not be able to understand or use it immediately, then six months or a year later the same thing comes up, and it not only makes sense, but fits a need.

2. The relationships you have built in the group are a source of joy and inspiration, to the extent you don't want to lose contact with these people who have meant so much to you. Many lasting friendships develop in support groups.

3. You are able to give back to others at least some of what you have received.

I am not sure where I would be in my journey if I hadn't started attending a support group. It has truly been a blessing in my life.

Journal Writing

Keeping a journal is an excellent way to capture your feelings, your sorrow, your pain, and the victories you experience on your journey. Journal writing has both short term and long term benefits. In the short term the journal provides a therapeutic value by helping you sort out the breadth and depth of your grief, and commit it to writing. In the long term it provides you with a historical reference of how far you have come on your journey.

Remember in Chapter 3 when I mentioned evaluating your progress at six month intervals? Well, a journal serves as an excellent tool for comparing where you are today with where you were then.

No rules govern how often you write, or what you write. The journal represents your personal account of your journey, and therefore you, and only you, should decide its content. It is private, so you should feel free to say what is in your heart. And quite frankly, the more candidly you write, the more helpful the exercise will be. Consult the Appendix for specifics on journal writing, and start yours today.

Humor

Over the course of our marriages most of us developed our own brand of humor. For some it was dry, for others boisterous. For some it involved telling funny stories, for others it involved practical jokes. For some it was spontaneous, for others it was contrived. In whatever forms, humor adds a very special quality to our lives.

Tools

Of one thing I am certain: the death of a spouse diminishes our ability to appreciate humor. Most persons find it extremely difficult to find humor in anything surrounding death, or the grief process. How do you laugh when you are crying?

Before you conclude that the question is odd, know that research shows that laughter is very therapeutic. The quicker you regain the ability to appreciate and participate in humorous events that occur, the quicker you will benefit from the healing power of humor and laughter.

You will restore your appreciation for humor when you recognize that the things that were humorous before your loss can still bring laughter today. Ask yourself: What did we laugh at together? Chances are the answer will be a particular television show or movie. Perhaps the things your children or grandchildren say and do. Maybe little things that co-workers, friends, or relatives said. Even little jokes you and your spouse played on each other. Any of these will bring a smile to your face, and yes, also a tear.

Many times the idea prevails that in mourning, laughter is taboo. Nothing could be further from the truth. Exercise good judgment, as there is a time and place for everything. However, no reasons exist to ignore humorous events because you have lost a spouse. I know, with certainty, that Jada would want and expect me to smile, laugh, and appreciate the humorous events that occur daily.

Many times the ability to find humor provides the strongest impetus for maintaining a sense of balance. And even in the darkest of times things can happen, or be said, that are so funny we have to laugh.

Take for example something that occurred on the night of Jada's death. My sister and I returned from the clinic in Tulsa, and throughout the trip my anxiety level mounted as I contemplated the most difficult thing I had ever attempted – telling our children that their mother had died.

As we entered the house the kids met us with joyous expressions, and asked where their mother was. I ushered them upstairs and proceeded to explain what had happened. Expectedly, emotions poured out immediately, and continued with alternating crying and talking. After about 30 minutes I knew we needed to take a break from this initial shock, but I was uncertain how to do this without appearing to shut off the need for more tears.

Out of the blue our youngest son, Chad, blurted out, "But Dad, this means you'll have to get remarried!" Now, this was not intended to be funny, but it caught everyone so off guard that we burst out laughing. I believe we gained two very valuable things from Chad's expression: we moved toward the break we needed, and I realized that even when everything appears bleak we can still appreciate the special gift of laughter.

Tools of the Intellectual Self

The tools of the intellectual self deal with learning – from others, from reading, from reflection. Intellect is not about being well-educated in a formal sense. These tools provide a way to seek insight and perspective, and then practice what you learn. It allows us to explore the breadth and depth of other tools, and can truly add meaning to our journey.

Several of the tools already covered, such as counseling, support groups, and scripture study could also be listed here, as they most certainly add knowledge. But, in pursuit of a different kind of insight, I offer two tools of a different nature: *reading, and alignment of beliefs and actions*.

Reading

The shelves of your local library and bookstores are loaded with volumes that can provide a broad range of insights. Some focus on spiritual gifts, others on life's lessons, some on specific topics, others quite general. Some will be clinical or research based, others will be about personal experience. Some will be short, others long.

Each individual is so different that recommending specific works becomes complicated. Still, I am sure that you can find a variety of titles that will meet your needs, and I have listed some possibilities in a bibliography at the end of the exercises in the Appendix.

I have been an avid reader for many years, particularly during travel on business. I tended to select books for entertainment and escapism, and I avoided self help books at all costs, viewing them the way I viewed counseling. I simply had no use for that type of reading, and, quite frankly, I perceived that the authors were simply preying on people's emotions. Even after Jada's death I saw little value in books of this nature.

How ironic that seems now. Here I am, writing the type of book I so steadfastly ignored. What caused me to change? Purely by accident I began reading the book, *The Seven Habits of Highly Effective People* by Stephen Covey.

About eight months after Jada's death our oldest son, Charlie, said he wanted money for his 17th birthday present rather than a specific gift. Although I didn't have a major problem with this I still felt the need to add something meaningful to it. I came up with the idea of buying Covey's book and putting half of Charlie's birthday money in the book's pages, along with a note expressing how proud I was of him, and that when he had read the book and could discuss it with me then

I would give him the other half of his birthday money.

About a week after his birthday I realized that I would be very hypo-critical, not to mention embarrassed, when we sat down to discuss the book and he discovered that I hadn't even read it. I rushed out for my own copy and began reading. To my surprise and amazement I found it filled with insights that helped me answer questions from my past, and to ask questions about my future. Much of what I read validated things I already knew, but with each chapter I discovered new ideas that, when reflected upon, began filling in gaps. My eyes had opened to new possibilities.

Covey's sequel, *First Things First*, added another layer of understanding, particularly in the identification of the most important things (first things) in my life. I realized a difference between what I said were the first things and what my actions demonstrated as the first things.

A decidedly spiritual tone and quality shone through both books, too, which worked well in conjunction with the spiritual tools.

Reading and rereading these books helped me gain greater insight into myself. As I put to use what I learned, merged with the spiritual tools, I gained clarity on what I had become, and how it differed from what I wanted to be. By reflecting on these learnings I began forging the new state of normalcy I both needed and wanted.

Alignment of Beliefs and Actions

Before discussing this tool I want to emphasize that it is more appropriate for those of you who have moved beyond the early stages of the grief process, to the stage of readiness for the creation of your new state of normalcy. I began exploring this concept shortly after the first anniversary of my loss, and it was truly a breakthrough discovery for me.

As I reflected on Covey's books I became aware of conflicts between what I said I believed, and how I acted. For example, I said that my family was more important than my work, yet for many years I had spent far more time at work than with my family. Even when I was home I was actually at work.

I said I believed that my spiritual growth and the spiritual growth of my children were important, yet my actions demonstrated the opposite. Time and time again I discovered inconsistencies that not only helped me understand many of my past failures, but more importantly helped me see the new path I both needed and wanted to travel.

I further enhanced this realignment exercise through exposure to Joel Barker on the subject of paradigms. Barker is a business consultant, and his book *Paradigms: The Business of Discovering the Future* is a business management book about change. Although I read it for business purposes, I found it equally useful in personal change, and if you think about it, there aren't too many people who undergo more change than surviving spouses.

Finally, as I sought full understanding of God's plan for me I saw that many of my personal characteristics had become stale. If I was to be successful in living God's plan I had to make some fundamental changes in the alignment of my beliefs and actions.

Tools of the Physical Self

Any discussion of the trauma on a surviving spouse invariably centers on the emotional impact. The trauma to the physical person is equally vital.

The grieving process, and the inevitable changes therein, exacts a heavy toll on the physical health, if neglected.

I could have placed the physical self in the chapter on traps, since failure to take care of yourself most definitely leads to major problems. But this vital step fits better as a good tool for restoration.

Telling you to take care of yourselves is nothing new. We all know what we should do. Ah, but doing it ... something else altogether. What can I say that you don't already know? I'll remind you of four very important points, and refer you to the exercises in the back of the book:

❖ Get enough rest. This is a must. Your body needs rest to face everyday challenges. In all likelihood your sleep patterns will be disrupted, and you will probably find that they change to some extent. If you find that you can't sleep, discuss it with your doctor for the best advice on what to do.

Too much sleep or the tendency to remain in bed can be a sign of depression, which, if left untreated, reaps devastating consequences. If you experience this, see your doctor immediately.

❖ Proper nutrition is a key ingredient in maintaining physical health. Most people struggle with this even when their spouse is alive, and unbalanced diet and bad eating habits become worse after their death. Consult a nutritionist, a home economist, or an extension service about nutrition, and receive help in planning a balanced diet that will meet your needs. Contact them without hesitation, and then use the information they provide.

❖ Exercise is a dirty word to some of us, but it can go a long way in preventing a number of potentially life-threatening conditions. Whether walking, running, swimming, or some other form, exercise improves your physical condition, even in small doses, plus your mental and emotional condition as well. Consult your physician before starting an exercise program.

❖ Regular check-ups by your doctor, dentist, and optometrist make up essential parts of maintaining the physical self, identifying health problems in their early and most treatable stages, and verifying the good behaviors you have committed to are achieving positive results.

A final tool that easily gets overlooked: yourself. Within everybody lies a strong-willed individual who is capable of doing just about anything within the laws of physics and physical limitations.

That strong will to survive, and to truly live again, drives you forward.

The soul would have no rainbow had the eyes no tears.

—John Vance Cheney

Chapter 9
Thoughts

Throughout the writing of this book, periodically I had thoughts and made notations of some random topics that didn't seem to fit smoothly in any of the chapters.

Rather than leave them out, or try to force them to fit somewhere awkwardly, they make for a tidy chapter on their own as we near the end of this journey together. Some stand simply on their own as statements; others will require explanation.

After the first thought, which definitely is the foremost, the others appear in no particular order of importance.

1. Let yourself grieve! The experience of losing a spouse hurts, and often times we think we can make the pain go away simply by going on with life as if nothing changed, pretending it doesn't hurt too much. Unfortunately, grief follows the line of a well-known television commercial: "You can pay me now, or pay me later." Grieve now, or grieve later, and if you choose later, then expect the

pain to be more intense than it is today. In other words, you will pay not just later, but more.

2. Lean into your discomfort. Most everything in the grief process creates discomfort and/or pain. A strong tendency is to avoid the pain, and sometimes that is absolutely the right thing to do. Nature has its way of taking care of us. But at some point in the process of rebuilding, pain has its place. Remember in Chapter 4 the discussion about facing situations that we know will cause emotional pain? Lean into it; approach the pain slowly, to test the water. I've found this works much better than a full-speed-ahead approach.

3. The grief process often feels like being caught on a giant roller coaster that never stops. The crawl to the crests, and the rushes into downward slopes, and the corkscrew turns many times are frightful and leave us breathless. But the hardest part of all is when the ride rolls on, and on, and on—and you take on the frustration of the seemingly endless journey. There is a tendency to fight it, to try to get off before it stops, indeed, sometimes even while the ride is still going full-steam. Doing so during the grief process is likely to create problems detrimental to your recovery. I am not saying sit back and enjoy the ride, for I know that is impossible. What I am saying is, take a deep breath and relax to whatever extent you can, and hold on tight. It does get better in time.

4. Nobody awards medals for being the best griever. Perhaps this sounds silly, but I was amazed at how easy it was to put on a happy face and pretend everything was going according to my plan. Many times I tried to hide my pain from those around me. How foolish I was! I was trying to get people to acknowledge my firm grasp on the situation. I perpetuated this lie for several months as I heard people say how proud they were of how I was handling everything.

I heard it so often that I began to believe that I had some special capability.

I should have had a cape. Super Griever, to the rescue. Who was I kidding? Myself, mostly. Fortunately I came to my senses about this damaging behavior. The moral: Be truthful to yourself. Let the world see your good days, and your bad.

The flip side of this coin is the development of a co-dependent need for others essentially to take care of your every need, both real and perceived. That is not healthy either.

5. Others say many things to you intended to bring comfort, but inadvertently are quite painful. And while you might agree with what someone says, their words in no way lessen your grief. Some of my favorites that I'm sure you have heard:

He/she is no longer suffering ... (and) is with God in heaven; you were fortunate to have had him/her for so long; it was a merciful death.

Hearing these things is not likely to bring you comfort in the early stages of your grief, the time you are most likely to hear them. However, keep in mind that comments of this nature are intended to provide comfort, not to be hurtful. Patience and understanding bode you well with those who choose to express themselves in this way.

6. Many have come before you. Seek them out and learn from them. Many will come after you. Teach them what you have learned.

7. Living in the past makes it impossible to see the possibilities of the future.

8. Throughout your journey the road will fork many times, and you must choose which path to take. One path always winds closer to your goal of recovery, others meander far astray. It is seldom obvious which is which. Choose wisely.

9. If you are not willing to fail then you reduce the likelihood of succeeding.

10. Keep your expectations realistic, none of us is perfect and we will make mistakes.

11. Three things matter most in life: *Faith, Family, and Friends.* Everything else is just window dressing. Certainly such matters as job security and financial security are important on some level, but when all is said and done they truly have very little significance.

Happiness is a do-it-yourself project.

—Wallene Dockery-Barzizza

Chapter 10
Living Again

Y ou and I began our journey in darkness, never knowing when or if we would see the light again. Our strongest hope was to make it through each day, to survive. As we proceeded through the grief process and our pain subsided, we realized that we had made it through the Black Forest, often without a compass.

We survived this terrible ordeal of losing a spouse to death. Unfortunately, many persons will stop at survival, thinking that once they take comfort in surviving, the rest will come automatically. Some even think they don't deserve anything more.

I believe we both deserve more, and we can have more, as long as we are willing to work for more (and only you can define what more is).

But first we must understand that living again is not about survival.

Many accept as a matter of faith the concept of spiritual life after death. We can't see it, we can't touch it, we can't hear it, yet in our heart of hearts we know it is there. Without a doubt. Why then, when we are so certain of this, do we struggle so hard with the concept of being able to live again after the loss of our spouse? Just as God has made spiritual life after death possible, so has He made life after death possible for the living.

The grief process tends to revolve around the past and the present (closing the door). The process of living again centers on the present and the future (opening new doors).

So, what does living again mean?

First it is about you, and no one else but you. I know that sounds self-centered, but this entire thesis is about your life and God's plan for it, about your happiness and fulfillment.

Neither the deceased spouse nor memories of her or him can be an active part of your living again. That is the primary reason I advocate the concept of ritualistically closing the door in Chapter 1.

Second, living again is about learning the use of, and then putting to use the tools described in Chapter 8. I cannot emphasize enough the importance of the spiritual tools and how they can lead you to an understanding of God's plan for your life.

Third, your journey is about change. Given an alternative, certainly we would not have selected this event for our spouses and ourselves, but it is the hand we have been dealt and we must choose either to play that hand or fold. Living again says to others and to ourselves that we choose to play. It's your deal now.

Finally, your renewed life is about discovery. You rediscover a peace and joy that we may have thought had vanished from our lives forever when we suffered our loss.

Living Again

You will discover once again the beauty of the world we live in, discovering that even though life will not be the same as it was before, your life still can be richly rewarding.

Living again is a metamorphosis, similar to that of a caterpillar. During the grieving process we resemble the caterpillar, just trying to survive. At the appropriate time we enter the cocoon and begin the metamorphosis, undergoing the most remarkable changes. When we are ready, and the time is right, we emerge from the cocoon as a new and unique form, ready to take our place in the world as a wondrous new re-creation –a butterfly, ready to spread wings and fly.

Many who travel this path would like the assurance of a step-by-step, formulaic process to follow, a recipe for success. Unfortunately, to my knowledge, no such recipe exists. At best, you can experience controlled trial and error. Like the early explorers who charted and mapped their way to and across this great country of ours, you can, at best, describe the basic lay of the land, identify the principle obstacles you will encounter, and list the provisions you will need for your journey. And as you prepare to embark, know that many have gone successfully before you, and through their thoughts and prayers stand ready to offer you support, just as you will stand ready in support of those who will follow you.

May God's Love and Blessing be with you and your family during every step of your journey.

Epilogue

Time marches on, and so does our recovery. Slowly, but surely we begin to see the light, and the life, at the end of the proverbial tunnel. Always getting better, our story continues toward no certain ending. And I believe with all my heart that this is how it should be, and will remain.

In a few weeks my family will again experience the anniversary of Jada's death. We no longer view that day with fear and anxiety, no longer anticipate with ever-increasing stress. The anniversary never will be forgotten or ignored. Some level of emotional response will always come attached to that date.

I have arrived, though, at a point in my recovery where I can acknowledge ceremoniously the anniversary of her death without being consumed by the power of its images. For now I am living again.

Just as the ordeal of Jada's death caused my world to crumble, the experience of grief recovery paved the way for me to rebuild my life. And to rebuild not to the same point, but a better point. The experiences of the last three years have shown me how to improve myself. I am a better person today than I was before Jada died. I am a better father, a better son, a better brother, and I will be a better husband.

Living Again

As I reflect on the three years that just passed I can see how each event, positive and negative, helped heal my wounded heart as I moved a little closer toward my new life.

God's hand has been on my shoulder throughout this journey, as He has been throughout my life: comforting me in times of extreme sadness and guiding me through the maze of doubt and uncertainty, challenging me to live my life according to His plan and showing me how to again love and be loved. And, finally, when I was ready, allowing Julie Williams, a wonderful, loving, caring woman into my life.

I can say without hesitation that Julie completes me, just as Jada completed me when we were married. God has blessed me with the love of two wonderful women.

My life did not end when Jada died. It took a detour. And after a bumpy start over the unpaved road of grief recovery I eventually emerged back on life's highway. It looks familiar in many ways, but somehow changed. What I realize is that life's highway hasn't changed.

I have.

Living Again Exercises

T hese exercises will help you put into perspective the feelings and emotions related to the loss of your spouse, and will provide the skills and motivation necessary to move you beyond your grief to the new state of normalcy I call living again. I believe that writing about the journey through grief provides a framework to build on. Repeat each exercise as often as you feel compelled to, for repeating the exercises adds breadth and depth to your story.

As you complete the exercises please keep in mind:

❖ Lean into any discomfort this experience causes.

❖ If the exercise suggests writing, but you would rather draw a picture, then draw a picture. If you do not want to write sentences and paragraphs, then simply write descriptive words or phrases. Do what is most comfortable for you – whatever allows you to capture your true feelings and emotions.

❖ Take ownership of what you write or draw. What I think, or your family thinks, or your minister, or anyone else, is unimportant.

❖ Write not just what you think, write what you feel, too.

❖ Use the blank pages for notes, feelings, concerns and questions as you go through the exercises.

Exercise 1
WHERE WILL YOUR STRENGTH COME FROM?

Your journey is both long and arduous. Abundant strength – spiritual, emotional, and physical – is essential to sustain perseverance. But, the journey has a way of depleting the needed strength, and frequently you must get a boost. Where will that boost of renewed strength come from?

Do the following every day:

Spiritual

Daily Prayer:

Lord, thank you for the blessings of life and for bringing me safely through another day. Give me the strength to meet all challenges that I encounter, the wisdom to seek and understand your plan for my life, and the courage to follow that plan.

Daily Scripture:

Reading scripture, or other meditative material of your choice, has a calming effect, and offers a reflective quality to the journey. When you read or what you read is less important than forming the habit that you read.

Daily Reflection:

Schedule some quiet time each day to consider God's presence, and how to serve Him. Also, at the end of the day, reflect on the events of that day to expand your perspective and prepare for meeting tomorrow's challenges.

Emotional

Daily hugs:

Get at least five hugs a day. I know this might be difficult for some men, but I can assure you that each hug will revitalize your reserves of strength.

Crying:

Cry as often as you need. Each episode will release your stored emotions.

Talk:

Talk as often as you can, daily if possible, about your loss, about your feelings, about your pain.

Daily Journal:

Writing down your feelings daily releases your thoughts and expands your ability to comprehend what is going on. Also, the journal provides a record of progress.

Obtain a notebook of blank pages that you will dedicate only to your daily journal writing. (Bookstores have a variety of journals especially designed for this task, or you can simply use notebooks from any school supply shelf.)

In capturing your thoughts and feelings, Rule No. 1 is: Keep it simple. Compose words and phrases in a random collection of your emotions and reflections on a given day. Journaling is not intended to be a diary of daily events, although certainly you can refer to them if they capture a significant thought or feeling.

Sometimes you capture what you would like to say to your lost spouse if she or he were with you.

Physical

Exercise:

Regular exercise is an essential part of physical well-being, and is an excellent release for the emotional stress that builds up in our bodies.

Diet:

Plan well-balanced meals. Avoid skipping meals. An uneven diet will affect your physical strength, which then drains energy emotionally and mentally.

Rest:

As quickly as possible get into a routine of going to sleep and getting up at the same time daily. Rest is an essential element of recovery.

Exercise 2
WHAT DO YOU NEED HELP WITH?

Identifying or admitting the need for help is one of your most difficult challenges. You will need the help of others. This exercise identifies some of the areas where you are likely to need that assistance. List your specific needs under each topic and who in your circle of family, friends, and acquaintances might be able to help.

NEED   WHO CAN HELP?
Spiritual:

1. _____   1. _____

2. _____   2. _____

3. _____   3. _____

Other: _____

_____

Emotional:

1. Someone to talk to anytime
   of the day, or night: 1. _____

2. Someone to count on
   when I am lonely: 2. _____

3. Someone I can cry with: 3. _____

Other: _____

_____

Physical:

1. Yardwork   1. _____

2. Home maintenance   2. _____

3. Housework   3. _____

4. Shopping   4. _____

5. Child care   5. _____

6. Transportation   6. _____

Other: _____

_____

Exercise 3
YOU AND YOUR LOSS

This exercise jump-starts a process of getting your true feelings and emotions out in the open. Describing what you feel about the loss of your spouse, and subsequently what you feel about yourself, is an important step. The tendency is a timid approach – passive words. Frank, open, even blunt description – revealing feelings and emotions for what they really are – allows you to process information for complete, healthy recovery.

Perform this exercise repeatedly. Each time, express yourself specifically and descriptively. If you are angry, how angry are you? Who or what are you angry at? If you are scared, what or who are you afraid of?

You cannot let go of these emotions unless you first let them out.

Describe how you feel about your loss: _____

_____

_____

_____

_____

_____

Describe how you feel about yourself: _____

_____

_____

_____

Exercise 4
WHAT ARE YOU AFRAID OF?

Throughout life you have had to confront fear, such as possible physical or emotional harm. The fear might have been real or imagined. Perceived fear is no less real; your perception is your reality. Each fear that arises represents a challenge or barrier that must be confronted in order to grow past it. Facing life after the loss of a loved one is one of those fears.

In this two-part exercise capture some of your past fears, from before your spouse died. How did you try to overcome your fear? Were you successful? Did the fear subside or go away? Focus on successes, times you stood up to your fear and conquered it.

In the second part capture the fears that have surfaced since your loss, and identify options for dealing with them.

Past Fears:

1. What was it? _____

    What did I do about it? _____

    _____

2. What was it? _____

    What did I do about it? _____

    _____

3. What was it? _____

    What did I do about it? _____

4. Others: _____

_____

Current Fears:

1. What is it? _____

   What might I do about it? _____

   _____

   _____

2. What is it? _____

   What might I do about it? _____

   _____

   _____

3. What is it? _____

   What might I do about it? _____

   _____

   _____

4. Others: _____

   _____

   _____

   _____

Exercise 5
WHAT WOULD THE DECEASED WANT FOR YOU?

Letting go completely of the past, and then moving into and embracing living again is one of the most difficult steps you must take. You might believe that experiencing happiness and joy might somehow reflect disrespect to the memory of your deceased wife or husband.

Deep down, you know what she or he would want for you as you move forward. Focus on three questions. The answers can open your eyes to a clear path toward living again.

What would the deceased want for you? _____

_____

_____

_____

How will you make this a reality? _____

_____

_____

_____

Would achieving this improve life as you know it today? How, specifically? _____

_____

_____

Exercise 6
BE KIND TO YOURSELF

Self-esteem and self confidence generally take a beating during grieving and recovery. Survival requires an abundance of both. Positive self-talk is critical. Awareness of limiters – known as self-limiting beliefs – is essential.

Why? Because you will stumble, and you must provide yourself with reinforcement. This is an area nobody can help you with, or do for you. The process is internal. The never-ending stream of challenges leads to inevitable mistakes and errors in judgment resulting in damage to self-esteem and self-confidence, which often are at a low ebb already. And, as if that is not enough, you add additional damage with negative self-talk or limiters.

Here's how to work on this liability:

Who talks to you more than anybody else? You do. Self-talk is almost constant. And you control all of the conversation. So, are you support-ive, kind, tactful to yourself? Or, do you beat yourself up for every little mistake or slip-up?

Limiters consist of self-imposed restrictions (usually in self-talk), and the key word is can't. You feel like you can't move on, and usually the words are something like: if only … I can't … I'll never. *Examples: If only Jada hadn't died, I would be OK. (This limits becoming OK.) I can't get over this.* Henry Ford said, *"If you believe you can, you're right. If you believe you can't, you're right."*

Describe how you use negative self talk: _____

_____

_____

How could you turn this negative into a positive? _____

_____

_____

_____

Describe how you use limiters: _____

_____

_____

_____

How could you turn this negative into a positive? _____

_____

_____

_____

Exercise 7
DOING WHAT'S MOST IMPORTANT

Life was never easy. Each day was packed with things to do, and never enough time to do them all. Then your husband or wife died. Your already overloaded schedule suddenly burst at the seams.

You now face enormous pressures with emotions running wild. Your internal circuitry is registering severe overload. And you don't have a big, red 'S' on your chest and Lois Lane on your arm.

Prioritize. Identify what is most important, and attend to it, first and foremost, without fail. Frustration mounts if you fall further and further behind. Take a hard look at what you are trying to accomplish and often you will find that every day is consumed by activity that doesn't really matter in the big picture or the long run.

Each year contains 52 weeks, each week 7 days, each day 24 hours, each hour 60 minutes. This is all we get. Make the most of it. A slogan to remember: Yesterday is a cancelled check. Tomorrow is a promissory note. Today is cash on hand; how do you want to spend it?

To create the most value from each day, focus your energy on tasks that you decide are most important to you and others who depend on you. Certainly situations urgent situations arise and require immediate attention. But, as self-improvement and time-management authority Stephen Covey of Franklin/Covey Inc. says, most of us spend far more time on what's urgent than on what's important. Allocate ample time every week for your most important priorities, and block out that time. Schedule it just as you would a work appointment (things like time with the children, time to exercise, etc.).

Not all the tasks that you want or need to have done have to be done today. What are the most important things in your life? Write them down first in the left-hand column, and then prioritize them:

Top 10 List	Top 10 List in Order of Importance
1.	1.
2.	2.
3.	3.
4.	4.
5.	5.
6.	6.
7.	7.
8.	8.
9.	9.
10.	10.

As you plan the day, the week, and the month follow this formula:

What has to be done today? Do it! _____

_____

_____

Living Again Exercises

What has to be done within the next week? Plan it! _____

_____

_____

_____

_____

_____

_____

What doesn't have to be done until next month? Hold it! _____

_____

_____

_____

_____

_____

_____

_____

Exercise 8
DEVELOPMENT OF IDENTITY

The death of your spouse created an abrupt and immediate alteration to your identity, much of which was defined by your marriage. The dissolution of that relationship frequently sends you spiraling into a crisis.

Two questions are important here: Who am I? Who do I want to become?

The search for and development of new identity is a large part of living again.

Describe your identity at three separate points – past, present, and future. Think deeply about this exercise, and reflect often on your responses. Write descriptively and specifically.

Who was I? _____

_____

_____

Who am I? _____

_____

_____

Who do I want to become? _____

_____

_____

Exercise 10
CELEBRATION

You will experience both failure and victory during your recovery journey through grief. Notice how quick you are to chastise yourself for your failures and human frailties, and how reluctant you are to celebrate victories.

As you slowly, but surely regain your life, each new discovery is a cause for celebration. Maybe your idea of celebrating is going out to dinner, or to a play. Maybe you would like a new article of clothing, or something for the house. What you treat yourself to is not nearly as important as treating yourself to something that has meaning and value to you.

Each celebration will build new positive memories as you begin living again.

How will you celebrate your victories? _____

_____

_____

_____

_____

_____

Suggested Reading

On Death and Dying, Elisabeth Kubler-Ross

Anticipatory Grief, Schoenberg, Carr, Kutscher, Peretz, and Goldberg

Remember, I Love You, Charlie W. Shedd

When Bad Things Happen to Good People, Harold Kushner

Widow, Lynn Caine

From a Healing Heart, Susan White-Bowden

Losing Someone You Love, Elizabeth Richter

How Do We Tell The Children, Dan Schaefer and Christine Lyons

A Grief Observed, C.S. Lewis

Good Grief, Granger E. Westberg

Facing Death, Billy Graham

The Jewish Way of Death and Dying, Maurice Lamm

The Christian Way of Death, Gladys Hunt

To Live Again, Catherine Marshall

The Seven Habits of Highly Effective People, Stephen R. Covey

First Things First, Stephen R. Covey, A. Roger Merrill, Rebecca R. Merrill

Exercise 9
POSSIBILITY THINKING

Possibility thinking is the opposite of the limiters in Exercise 6. By exploring possibilities you acknowledge that a bright future lies on the horizon. This step enables the development of focused plans for the future that signals the transition from grief recovery to the exciting world of living again.

What is the one thing (within the laws of physics and personal capability) that you believe you can't do today, but if you could, it would make a significant impact of your life?

_____

_____

_____

What would you have to do differently to be able to make this a reality?

_____

_____

_____

Who could help you?

_____

_____

_____